Building Landmarks, Smoothing Out Markets

A WORLD BANK STUDY

Building Landmarks, Smoothing Out Markets

An Enhanced Competition Framework in Romania

Arabela Aprahamian and Georgiana Pop, Editors

WORLD BANK GROUP

Contents

Boxes

Figures

Tables

Acknowledgments

The Advisory Services for the Romanian Competition Council (RCC) were performed by a World Bank Group team led by Arabela Aprahamian (Senior Operation Officer). The core team included Georgiana Pop (Senior Economist, Competition Policy Team) and Luisita Guanlao (Lead Information Officer) (both acting also as technical leaders), Graciela Miralles Murciego (Competition Specialist, Competition Policy Team), Denisa Popescu (Senior IT Officer), Steven Reichenbach (Consultant), Alexandru Stanescu (Operation Analyst), Ronald Myers (Senior Governance Consultant), Gonçalo Coelho (Competition Consultant, Competition Policy Team), Cesar Chaparro Yedro (Private Sector Development Specialist), and George Moldoveanu (Project Assistant). The extensive project team includes international and local experts (appendix A) from various communities of practices and organizations. Essential support was provided by Corina Grigore (Operations Officer), Oana Caraba (Consultant), Tanta Duta (Resource Management Analyst), Monica Ion (Accounting Assistant), Daniel Kozak (Communication Officer), and Ana Florina Pirlea (Private Sector Development Analyst).

The assistance benefited from valuable technical leadership on competition framework from Martha Martinez Licetti (Senior Economist, Global Competition Policy Team Lead) and on enterprise architecture from Arthur Riel (Director, Middleware Engineering). The team is also grateful for management strategic advice provided by Mamta Murthi (Country Director), Paloma Anos Casero (Practice Manager), Elisabetta Capannelli (Romania and Hungary Country Manager), Aurora Ferrari (Practice Manager, former Sector Manager), Isfandyar Zaman Kahn (Program Leader), Donato De Rosa (Senior Economist, former Task Manager), and Lalit Raina (Advisor, former Sector Manager).

We would like to thank President Bogdan Marius Chiritoiu, RCC Board members, and the directors and staff who have worked tirelessly with us on this project. The project management unit, led by Oana Neg (RCC Project Manager), has been a constructive and reliable partner in the implementation of this ambitious project. The RCC's feedback has been invaluable, and we appreciate all of the time and effort that the management and staff have devoted to this exercise.

Such substantial engagement could not have been successful without a coordinated collaboration both internally, within the World Bank Group, and externally, through leveraged collaboration with other international organizations, including the European Commission and the Organisation for Economic Co-operation and Development (OECD). Special thanks to ACM Netherlands, U.S. Department of Justice, U.S. Federal Bureau of Investigation, Bundeskartellamt of Germany, Competition Bureau of Canada, and Israel Competition Agency, all of which supported the project by sharing their best practices in the field of competition enforcement. Distinguished professors provided advice and shared experience from the following universities: King's College London, United Kingdom; University of Applied Sciences, Offenburg, Germany; Instituto de Empresa Business School, Spain; New York University, Stern Business School, United States; Leuven University, the Netherlands; Radboud University, Nijmegen, the Netherlands; Université Paris Ouest Nanterre La Défense, France; Oetovos Lorand University, Hungary; Utrecht University, the Netherlands; Leeds University, United Kingdom; Szeged University, Hungary; European University Institute of Florence, Italy; ASEBUSS—The Institute for Business Administration in Bucharest, Romania; University of Glasgow, United Kingdom; and University of Bucharest Law Faculty, Romania. The strengthened collaboration of the Romanian business community (through the coalition of AmCham Romania, Romanian Business Leaders, the Foreign Investment Council, and The Businessmen's Association of Romania) was very important for the invaluable feedback it provided on the business environment challenges to competition policy in Romania.

The main author of this report is Georgiana Pop, with contributions from Arabela Aprahamian, Alexandru Stanescu, Gonçalo Coelho, Luisita Guanlao, and Graciella Murciego. Helpful comments and advice were provided by peer reviewers Martha Martinez Licetti, Arthur Riel, Doerte Doemeland (Lead Economist, Romania Country Economist), Elisabetta Righini (Visiting Professor, Centre of European Law, King's College London), and Aurelian Dochia (Senior Economic Advisor for OECD, the World Bank, and the European Bank for Reconstruction and Development). Communications Development Inc., led by Bruce Ross-Larson with Maximillian Ashwill and Joe Caponio, provided editorial support.

The report provides an overview of the multitude of technical reports, training, and advocacy documentation for training sessions and advocacy events. Appendix B provides the list of deliverables under this Advisory Services team.

Executive Summary

Introduction

Romania identified competition as key to its effective economic development and is positioning the Romania Competition Council (RCC) to become more visible and effective. Improving Romania's competitive environment will attract new firms, weed out inefficient ones, and enhance growth potential. Just prior to the 2008 global financial crisis, Romania's economic growth rate was one of the fastest in the European Union (EU). After the crisis, Romania's growth stagnated, even recording negative rates in 2009 and 2010. The need to improve market functioning thus became even more important. Romania's competitive environment was found to be less dynamic than that of other EU countries because of restrictive regulations, barriers to foreign direct investment, and widespread state participation in the market.

An effective competition strategy leads to success in Romania's domestic market efficiency, economic growth, and European market integration. By improving the efficiency of national markets, competition policy contributes to a country's international competitiveness. Firms faced with robust competition have strong incentives to innovate, reduce costs, and become more efficient and productive than their rivals. Moreover, firms usually find many of their inputs (raw materials, energy, telecommunication services, and construction services) in local markets. If these local markets lack competition, the goods and services necessary for production are not competitively priced. As a result, the economy as a whole may become less competitive and less able to compete globally.

In Romania, the RCC is charged with guaranteeing market competition, enforcing compliance with laws governing competition, ensuring that state aid meets the rigorous EU criteria without creating market distortions, and promoting a broader understanding of the rules and benefits of competition. It has made good progress toward its goal of measuring up to EU standards and compares favorably with other EU nations. It has initiated far-reaching internal reforms to increase its effectiveness. It has begun to define a strategy to enhance performance and has taken steps to improve an overly rigid public administration system. And it has committed itself to becoming a center of excellence within Romania's public administration.

The Romanian government requested assistance from the World Bank Group to develop reforms to enhance Romania's competition culture and the

RCC's role as a competition advocate. Following a comprehensive functional review of the Romanian Competition Council carried out by the World Bank in 2010, weaknesses, needs, and priorities were identified. On the basis of recommendations in the review, the RCC and the government endorsed a Reform Action Plan (2012) that proposed a strategy to strengthen Romania's competitive framework. To help put this Action Plan into practice, the World Bank, under the Advisory Services, implemented an innovative delivery model that involved integrated expertise to (i) review the legal and regulatory framework for competition that required knowledge of the EU's legal and institutional framework and case law; (ii) offer advocacy support to streamline competition policy principles with other governmental policies and strengthen intergovernmental relations, especially with sectoral regulators (electricity and telecommunications) and the prosecutor's office; (iii) provide state-of-the-art capacity building to strengthen the RCC staff's technical knowledge and interactively design and implement a training program consistent with RCC goals; and (iv) optimize internal procedures to improve institutional functioning using Enterprise Architecture methodology, which provides an in-depth institutional assessment of the RCC and the development of a target business and information technology (IT) architecture.

Enforcement of Antitrust Rules

The World Bank's 2010 Functional Review highlighted the RCC's low cartel enforcement track record and the lengthy periods required to conclude competition cases. These were the result of, among other things, a legal framework that limited the RCC to effectively use its resources by prioritizing public interest cases aligned with its priorities; a leniency program that was not fully fledged and in which leniency applicants were not exempted from potential criminal prosecution; and a limited ability to negotiate the overall amount of the fine in settlements. Adding to these specific enforcement pitfalls, the RCC possessed a governance structure that relied too heavily on decisions being taken by the RCC's president. The competition law also established a set of burdensome rules in terms of merger review procedures and confidentiality of information, which ended up clogging the agency's ability to perform in a timely and effective manner.

To address these shortcomings, the RAS proposed a series of amendments to strengthen enforcement of the competition law and to empower the RCC to tackle the anticompetitive agreements and mergers that have the most distortive effects in the markets. To increase the overall effectiveness of the Romanian Competition Law (RCL), the World Bank proposed changes to enhance the RCC's procedural effectiveness through de-judicializing competition enforcement and to streamline fast-track procedures for less important mergers; to hire a hearing officer to deal with confidential matters that were a competence of the RCC president; and to assign some of the president's day-to-day operations to a neutral registry. The proposals also focused on the undue burdens imposed by the competition law on the private sector—suggesting elimination of the 40 percent presumption of dominance and its high minimum fines, as well as of the government's power to impose price controls. To make the RCC more agile and efficient, the World Bank also proposed several practical recommendations clarifying the confidentiality and access to file regimes and setting clear deadlines for the RCC, while limiting the parties' ability to engage in dilatory tactics. To articulate the proposed changes to the competition legal framework, the World Bank supported an advocacy event on the application of EU competition law in Romania, and training workshops on Comparative Competition Jurisprudence in EU Law and the key Principles of Competition law.

To help improve the effectiveness of antitrust enforcement, the World Bank proposed further changes to RCC's leniency regulations to increase legal certainty for leniency applicants and to refine the design of the leniency program, by limiting leniency to hard-core cartels, restructuring the existing provisions to allow for easy and quick identification of the main elements of the leniency program, and to establish stricter and clearer leniency requirements. Together with these proposed changes, the World Bank conducted advocacy events on IT forensics, cartel detection, and investigative techniques; the World Bank also promoted an outreach advocacy event to raise private sector awareness of competition law compliance and leniency programs. Consistent with these changes, suggestions were also made to improve the RCC's enforcement and sanctioning powers. Moreover, the World Bank produced comments on the "Comments to the Romanian 2010 Commitment Guidelines," proposing a new settlement regime allowing the RCC to agree with the violators on the amount of the fine in cases where they confess their guilt and are willing to pay a fine. Finally, to provide the RCC with the tools to produce sound decisions, the World Bank created a guide analyzing the effects of abuse of dominance on consumers, which draws on the EU legal framework and international best practices, and promoted two training sessions on economic research and analysis for the RCC staff.

Although merger review is at the core of the competition law enforcement, the RCC has not systematically conducted advanced economic analysis in cases that have a higher likelihood of affecting competition and consumers. In fact, the RCC's resources have been depleted by analyses of cases unlikely to affect competition because of the RCL's low merger notification thresholds and its lack of official merger notification forms, guidance on prenotification contacts, and clear and transparent confidentiality policies. From an analytical perspective, the RCC often failed to properly define relevant markets, which limited its ability to assess the actual impact of the mergers.

In response to these shortcomings, the World Bank proposed several modifications to the merger control framework: removing merger thresholds from the RCL; setting merger filing thresholds that ensure merging parties are of a significant size; reviewing merger thresholds on a regular basis; enhancing the scope and functioning of the fast-track procedure for merger notification; eliminating the assessment of whether a merger constitutes a threat to national security; consolidating RCC requests for information from parties during the merger review; formulating information requests proportionate to the complexity of the analysis to avoid generating unduly large costs for businesses; strengthening prenotification consultations; adopting clearer filing forms; and implementing more transparent confidentiality policies. To enable the adoption of sound decisions, the World Bank supported the design of a guide on the economic analysis of mergers, and another guide on the use of quantitative tools in market definition beyond merger control that offer key instruments for all types of competition law analysis. As a complement, the training session on economic research and analysis for RCC staff covered several aspects of merger control.

The RCC has already implemented some of the RAS recommendations on the competition legal framework. *A new draft competition law is being prepared*, which considers several RAS recommendations, such as removing merger thresholds from the RCL and including them in merger regulations that can be more easily updated; eliminating the 40 percent threshold for the presumption of dominance; removing price-control provisions; limiting the parties' right to challenge access to file and confidentiality before the courts and creating the salaried position of Independent Procedural Officer specializing in the disposition of access to file, confidentiality, and other procedural matters separate from the enforcement team within the RCC.

In addition to the proposed changes to the RCL, *new leniency guidelines have already been approved* by the RCC Board and cleared by the Legislative Council. But their adoption has been postponed due to legal issues concerning pending cartel cases that need to be addressed. The cartel-screening techniques were adapted and used by the RCC Economic Analysis Group in two separate projects: an internal guide for market screening and a market behavior analysis of beer producers in Romania for a beer market inquiry.

Finally, *modified commitment instructions were approved*, enabling the RCC to agree with violators on the amount of fines in cases where they acknowledge their anticompetitive conduct and are willing to accept a fine (with some bargaining possible on its amount). In line with the RAS proposals, *a new merger regulation was adopted on September 30, 2014*. This places a greater emphasis on prior contacts between the RCC and the merging parties; extends the scope of simplified procedures; and increases the RCC's transparency by publishing information on all merger notifications, allowing stakeholders to express their views. Furthermore, more efficient use of fast-track procedures has resulted in an average length of 1.8 months to complete a merger case in 2014, which represents a 23 percent decrease in the amount of time required compared to 2013.

State Aid Control

Given the widespread presence of state-owned enterprises (SOEs) in the Romanian markets and recurrent state aid many of them have received, upgrading Romania's state aid rules was identified as one of the key areas to prevent market distortions and eliminate administrative discretion. The European Commission has exclusive competence to assess the compatibility of proposed state aid measures with the internal market. However, the Commission and Member States share the responsibility for ensuring that EU state aid procedures work. The application of EU state aid rules within the different Member States, including Romania, requires the implementation of certain internal procedural rules, and EU law only requires that these internal rules ensure the good functioning of the EU state aid system. Romania's state aid regulatory framework required further alignment with the EU law. In particular, there was no reference to the role of national courts in state aid cases, and a lack of clarity in terms of ex ante cost-benefit analysis and ex post monitoring of state aid. In the RAS, the World Bank presented a proposal with modifications aimed at strengthening the state aid regulatory framework. The recommendations included clarifying the obligations of granting authorities and state aid beneficiaries, clarifying the procedural rules applicable to block-exempted state aid, developing the regulation of the recovery process concerning unlawful aid, ensuring transparency in the award of state aid to companies that perform services of general economic interest, clarifying the role of national courts in state aid cases, and raising state aid awareness and devoting sufficient resources to the RCC on state aid matters. Second, the World Bank developed a methodological guide to advise the different granting authorities on how to carry out ex ante and ex post assessments of state aid measures. The World Bank also provided comments to a draft ordinance on state aid procedural rules. The World Bank promoted an advocacy event on the EU state Aid Modernization reform to clarify the impact of the new rules in Romania, especially in relation to a single national contact authority, providing advice and special assistance to national authorities and beneficiaries, dialoguing with the European Commission, providing reports to the government, and collaborating with other national authorities in cases before the EU Court of Justice.

Concerning state aid, the RAS recommendations materialized through the adoption of the Emergency Ordinance 77/2014 on state aid national procedures, which clarifies information related to state aid notification, obligations of state aid granting authorities, aid recovery, the role of national courts, and de minimis aid.[1]

Unfair Competition Law

Given the RCC's new competences in the application of the unfair competition law, one of the main setbacks was the lack of clarity and predictability in the RCC's enforcement of Romania's Unfair Competition law, which resulted in an inefficient use of the RCC's resources and in higher costs for businesses. This stemmed from the RCC's lack of power to prioritize cases and from a legal framework that overlapped with other legal regimes and created several competence gaps. To address these issues, the World Bank prepared recommendations to amend the Romanian Unfair Competition Law, proposing the applicability of the law to all business-to-business activities and introducing a rule allowing the prioritization of cases by the RCC on the basis of a de minimis and an opportunity test. The World Bank conducted two advocacy events in which the proposed changes to the Unfair Competition Law were explained and held a training workshop on key principles of the Unfair Competition law.

The RAS recommendations were incorporated into a Government Ordinance in December 2014. This Ordinance (adopted in August 2014), which modified Romania's Unfair Competition Law, incorporates an opportunity test to trigger the RCC's competence based on public interest and the degree to which the market structure is affected, and it will apply to all activities. Furthermore, the RCC adopted a Procedural Regulation in November 2014, which clarified issues regarding the application of the opportunity test and the capacity to file complaints with the RCC.

Sectoral Issues

Despite the various reforms, Romania's railways sector remained plagued with inefficiency. The World Bank recommended that Romania should deepen the liberalization of the sector by more efficiently separating infrastructure from railways services and by bringing this sector's regulation fully in line with EU law by implementing key aspects of the EU Recast Directive. The main recommendations focused on extending the powers and competences of the Railways Supervisory Council (RSC), extending the services to be provided by the infrastructure manager, increasing transparency upon entrance to the railway market, strengthening the financial structure of the railways sector, and requiring more accurate infrastructure charging rules by providing further guidance on the determination of compensation for public service contracts. Following these recommendations, *the RSC has already endorsed, together with the Ministry of Justice, a draft law initiated by the Ministry of Transport that will implement the EU Recast Directive.*

In the communications area, Romania lacked a clear set of rules governing state aid for broadband network deployment, which unduly increases the risk of market distortions and may crowd out private investment. To fill this gap, the World Bank developed an internal guidance for the RCC recommending that public support not undermine the private sector's incentives to invest by focusing on those areas where market operators have already invested or would normally choose to invest; that open access to broadband infrastructure should be promoted to foster downstream competition; and that alternative means of support that do not amount to state aid should be favored to lower the administrative burdens incurred. Following the RAS recommendations, *the RCC approved guidelines to assess public support for deploying broadband network infrastructure in 2014.*

Further, a gap was identified in analyzing network-sharing agreements, notably in the process of balancing their pro-competitive and anti-competitive effects. The World Bank developed guidelines to help the RCC and the Romanian Telecommunications Regulator ascertain how competition rules are applied to network-sharing agreements. The guidelines analyze the implications of infrastructure-sharing agreements in light of the degree of cooperation between the parties: typically, passive infrastructure-sharing agreements raise fewer competition concerns than active sharing because they do not require the sharing of network elements, do not result in the high commonality of costs, and do not involve significant information and forecasting exchanges between competitors. Second, in active infrastructure agreements the degree of cooperation increases, which raises the risk of collusion. *In 2014, the RCC published guidelines on network-sharing agreements, building on the RAS results and offering a framework for the assessment of passive and active infrastructure sharing.*

The high risk of collusion in public procurement highlighted the need to make public procurement pro-competitive at all levels to minimize unnecessary budget costs. In practice, there was a need to develop clear guidance for the public procurement specialists on how to design pro-competitive tenders to enhance competition among bidders and reduce the risks of bid rigging. The World Bank promoted an advocacy event on bid-ridding detection techniques and provided guidelines targeting contracting authorities. These guidelines offer detailed practical advice on each of the procurement phases: prebidding, bidding design, bidding stage, and postbidding, to mitigate restrictions of competition throughout the entire procurement cycle.

The 2010 Functional Review also highlighted the need to embed competition principles in sectoral policies through closer collaboration between the RCC and sector regulators. While the RCC had protocols of collaboration with sector regulators (telecommunications, electricity, consumer protection, pharmaceuticals, public procurement, public utilities, and financial sectors), these remained ineffective due to the absence of full-fledged action plans for their implementation in day-to-day work. In particular, there was no model protocol with companion material, such as a checklist to spot suspicious behavior related to anticompetitive practices, a list of indicators to monitor effective market competition, and questionnaires to assess if proposed regulations could have negative effects on competition. To address these concerns, the World Bank proposed revising the existing protocols signed by the RCC, providing guidance on how to enhance consultation mechanisms in the context of merger analysis, state aid, and unfair commercial practices; consistent procedural rules, forbearance, confidentiality, information sharing, periodical meetings, focal points, confidentiality, allocation of cases, and transfer of cases to the competent authority; and a periodical review to ensure that the content of the protocol is current and that the parties maintain an interest in its implementation. *Five out of 10 collaboration protocols with sector regulators are already signed and in force.*

Operational Framework, Institutional Governance, and Human Resources

The 2010 Functional Review identified several shortcomings of the RCC's internal business architecture and information technology environment. These were mainly related to the RCC's limited operational effectiveness and complex organizational processes, misalignment of the staff's roles with institutional objectives, bundling of investigative and decision-making functions, and absence of clear rules for accountability. Technology-wise, the RCC's incomplete architecture manifests itself by a generalized minimal use of IT tools across the RCC and the absence of IT strategies, principles, processes, or architectures to define how IT can be leveraged to support business operations. In a nutshell, the RCC's organization was limiting its ability to fulfill core functions.

To overcome these concerns, the World Bank proposed several measures aimed at improving internal and external transparency and visibility; enhancing operational effectiveness through the development of a coherent strategy and simplified organizational processes; aligning the roles of staff with institutional objectives; separating investigative from adjudicative functions; providing clear rules for accountability; pushing responsibilities to the lowest operational level; and developing an IT strategy that is aligned with institutional priorities. A phased approach to four core reform areas (strategy, governance, mandated functions, and technology) was recommended and synthesized in a migration plan. The business architecture objectives were solidified with a series of training sessions to strengthen RCC officials' competencies in terms of effective written communications, people management and communication, leadership and problem solving, competition project management, and strategy formulation and change management.

Following the RAS recommendations, the RCC has already implemented a series of business architecture reforms. The distribution of workloads began in accordance with predetermined criteria; accountability is delegated to the lowest level in the process; standardized checklists and forms are implemented to promote consistency across the RCC. IT forensics was strengthened with new technologies and mandatory training in the use of these technologies. Streamlining the RCC's functions included the implementation of the first phase of business reengineering, the automation of the mergers processes, and the development of foundational software solutions to support the execution and monitoring of RCC operations, while starting plans for the implementation of the last two phases.

Finally, several gaps were identified regarding the RCC's human resources. As highlighted in the 2010 Functional Review, there was a need to improve the management of human resources and the internal agency. Overall, the RCC lacked a structured approach to staff planning linked to strategy, relied on recruitment and selection processes that are not fully efficient, and had a system of grade promotion that was not conducive to adequate performance. To address these issues, the World Bank proposed various measures to strengthen the recruitment and selection processes, use key performance indicators for the recruitment process, create greater transparency in the process of grade promotion, build a set of performance indicators, and improve processes for setting staff objectives and performance evaluation and align them with the RCC's mission.

Since 2014, the RCC has been implementing improved techniques for human resource management. The induction of newly recruited officers led to faster integration of human resources into the RCC activity, and internships were used to screen talent. Staff promotion was made more dynamic by basing it on performance, with an increased number of promotions in 2013 over the previous years. Desired competencies were introduced for teamwork, conflict management, decision making, and problem solving; planning, organizing, and managing projects for external relations and support departments; legal competition framework; and planning and organizing for management staff.

Moving Forward

The RAS delivered on the three main areas included in the Reform Action Plan (2012) to strengthen Romania's competition framework: (i) the RCC internal restructuring to move personnel and resources to the frontline of competition enforcement; (ii) the RCC mission and strategy coherent strategy backed by results indicators; and (iii) the RCC accountability, modernization of merit-based human resource management, and modern information technology and communication infrastructure. Further, the RCC has already begun using some of the tools acquired under the RAS in ongoing cases (see box ES.1).

Nevertheless, there is an unfinished agenda that requires further implementation of RAS recommendations and competition reforms.

- Concerning *state aid*, further work is required to reduce competition distortions stemming from unlawful state aid, especially in terms of assessing impact, collecting data to raise transparency, reporting state aid to the European Commission, and raising awareness of granting authorities.
- Regarding the *unfair competition law*, a monitoring and evaluation mechanism could be developed to assess the effectiveness of the RCC's enforcement and the court's case law.
- Concerning the RCC's *business architecture*, the automation of the sector inquiries, unfair competition, antitrust activities, and regulatory impact assessments should be prioritized and sequenced in an implementation plan. Also, development of "big data" technologies—for example, analyzing procurement patterns to identify bid rigging—should enable the RCC to foster competition more effectively.
- *Management* of *human resources and finances* must be regularly addressed as in the past. The impact assessment of the RAS training program identified

opportunities to address persistent skill deficiencies. One type of training would focus on improving the RCC's capacity to conduct evidence-based analysis. A second type would support efforts to improve the regulation of certain sectors of the economy. A third type would help relevant RCC staff to lead and manage teams. A fourth type would help this staff to effectively communicate and represent the RCC to stakeholders and the public.

• *Finalizing the new IT architecture that modernizes the RCC's digital efforts is a priority.* The RCC's *mission, vision, and strategic goals* will be championed to maintain staff motivation and enthusiasm. Competency-based staffing policies will be implemented, including competency-related key performance indicators, as part of annual performance evaluations. A formal mentoring program and developmental assignments will encourage on-the-job training.

Box ES.1 Application of RAS Results

The RCC has increased its focus on cartel detection and bid-rigging practices in public procurement. In 2014, 44 percent of the major investigations concluded by the RCC and the majority of the new investigations opened (34 percent) concerned cartels. In addition, a platform for whistleblowers who wish to provide anonymous relevant information on cartels was created. Between 2013 and 2015, the RCC opened seven new cartel investigations in financial services, cereal, film distribution, and IT markets, as well as five new bid-rigging cases in the public procurement[2] of dairy products to schools and of gas connection and upgrading and maintenance work for related facilities. Relevant to targeted training on cartel investigation techniques, detection of bid rigging in public procurement, and compliance with competition law and leniency policy, the RCC staff would be better equipped to perform dawn raids at firms' headquarters to find evidence of collusive behavior and to analyze evidence of price agreements. The RCC also transposed the cartel-screening techniques learned during the advocacy event on prevention and detection of bid rigging in public procurement into an internal guide on market screening and applied them to a market analysis of beer producers in Romania for an inquiry about the beer market.

Acquired economic analysis and legal skills would also help the RCC staff to analyze the effects of three new cases of abuse of dominance opened during 2013–15 and affecting consumers in several markets (pharmaceutical supply, electricity meter devices, and marketing of television channels) and also help the staff to perform competition assessments of several markets (pharmaceuticals, communications, wood, health care, auto insurance, and insolvency lawyers) during eight market inquiries opened in the same period. Similarly, the acquired skills would aid the review process of five new vertical agreement cases opened in the same period (in the areas of food retail, film distribution, batteries and accumulators, and electricity meter devices) and aid merger review. Finally, in 2014, the RCC authorized 42 mergers, half of them conducted according to a simplified procedure

box continues next page

Box ES.1 **Application of RAS Results** *(continued)*

(for example, in financial services; production and marketing of wood tar, preforms and bottles, natural gas and electricity; sugar production; and media and advertising). The average time required for the merger cases to be completed was 1.81 months, 23 percent less than the time recorded in 2013.

Regarding state aid control, the guidelines on public support for the extension of broadband infrastructure have already improved methods of analysis of state aid elements related to the Ro-Net project, which examines the development of broadband communication infrastructure in disadvantaged areas.

Source: Romanian Competition Council, www.consiliulconcurentei.ro.

Notes

1. To simplify state aid control, certain categories of state aid must not be reported to the Commission prior to their implementation. The European Council adopted the Enabling Regulation, allowing the European Commission to adopt block exemption Regulations (Council Regulation (EC) No 994/98 of May 7, 1998, on the application of Articles 92 and 93 of the Treaty establishing the European Community to certain categories of horizontal state aid. OJ L 142, 14.05(1)998, pages 1–4). According to the block exemption Regulation, the state aid measure (whether a scheme or individual aid) is declared compatible with the internal market without the need to notify it, provided that the measure in question complies with all of the conditions laid down in the Regulation. De minimis aid falls below a threshold established in the legislation (EUR200,000) and should not be reported to the European Commission.

2. In 2012, the RCC opened four bid-rigging investigations into several public procurement procedures (representing 22 percent of the total number of investigations on the possible infringement of the competition law) and three cartel investigations (Romanian Competition Council, Annual Report 2012).

Abbreviations

ACP	Authority for Certifications and Payments
ANCOM	National Authority for Communication
ANFP	National Agency of Public Function
ANM	National Agency for Medicine
ANPC	National Consumer Protection Authority
ANRMAP	National Regulatory Authority for Public Procurement
ANRSC	National Regulatory Authority for Municipal Services
ASF	Authority for Financial Supervision
CAT	Competency Architect Tool
CNMSI	National Management Centre for the Informational Society
CNSC	National Council for Solving Complaints
DLAF	Fight against Fraud Department
DoJ	Department of Justice
EA	Enterprise Architecture
EU	European Union
FDI	foreign direct investment
GDP	gross domestic product
GoR	Government of Romania
IT	information technology
MA	Managing Authority
NMA	The Netherlands Competition Authority
OECD	Organisation for Economic Co-operation and Development
PMR	Product Market Regulation
PPP	purchasing power parity
RACI	Responsible, Accountable, Consulted, Informed
RAS	Romania Spatial and Urban Strategy Reimbursable Advisory Service
RCC	Romania Competition Council
RCL	Romanian Competition law

RSC	Railways Supervisory Council
SAM	State Aid Modernization
SGEI	services of general economic interest
SOE	state-operated enterprises
TFEU	Treaty on the Functioning of the European Union
TFP	total factor productivity
TOGAF	The Open Group Architecture Framework
UCVAP	Unit for Coordinating and Verifying Public Procurement

CHAPTER 1

Context

Introduction

Romania made significant progress in opening its markets to competition and integrating its economy with the European Union (EU)'s internal market. In preparation for EU accession in 2007, Romania was one of the fastest reforming countries in Europe. The reforms were driven by requirements to bring national laws in line with existing EU norms and regulations that form the *acquis communautaire*. The goal of the reforms was to adjust regulations to make Romania's regulatory framework consistent with that of the EU and its competitive market economy. These made it easier for businesses to get credit, employ workers, protect investors, obtain licenses, and trade across borders and close down. But after EU accession in 2007, Romania suffered from "reform fatigue," and many planned reforms were never accomplished. This reversal was most apparent in the energy and transport sectors and in projects to modernize state institutions (World Bank 2013).

Romania's growth reveals a vulnerable competitive environment and the need to enhance its export competitiveness in order to achieve greater economic convergence with the rest of the EU. Per capita gross domestic product (GDP) increased from 31 percent of the European average in 2000 to 55 percent in 2014 (IMF 2014). Much of this growth was driven by a reallocation of labor from less productive sectors like agriculture, to more productive sectors like services and construction. The global financial crisis of 2008 stalled Romania's economic growth. In 2009, Romania's economy contracted by a stunning 6.6 percent; in 2010, it contracted by 1.5 percent. More recently, Romania's economy has slowly begun to recover from the economic crisis of 2008. In 2014, Romania recorded one of the highest GDP growth rates in the EU at 2.4 percent. This placed GDP per capita at about half of the EU average in 2014. According to the World Bank (2013a), this growth was driven by export performance and a strong year for agriculture.[1] However, Romania's competitive environment still compares unfavorably with that of other EU countries—for several reasons, notably restrictive regulations, barriers to foreign direct investment (FDI), and widespread state participation in the market (box 1.1).

Box 1.1 Restrictiveness of Product Market Regulations in Romania

Product market regulations in Romania are among the most restrictive in the EU. On the basis of the OECD's Product Market Regulation (PMR),[a] Romania ranked as the 20th most restrictive country in competition, of 22 EU countries in 2011 (figure B1.1.1).

Figure B1.1.1   Product Market Regulation: Romania Compared with EU Countries

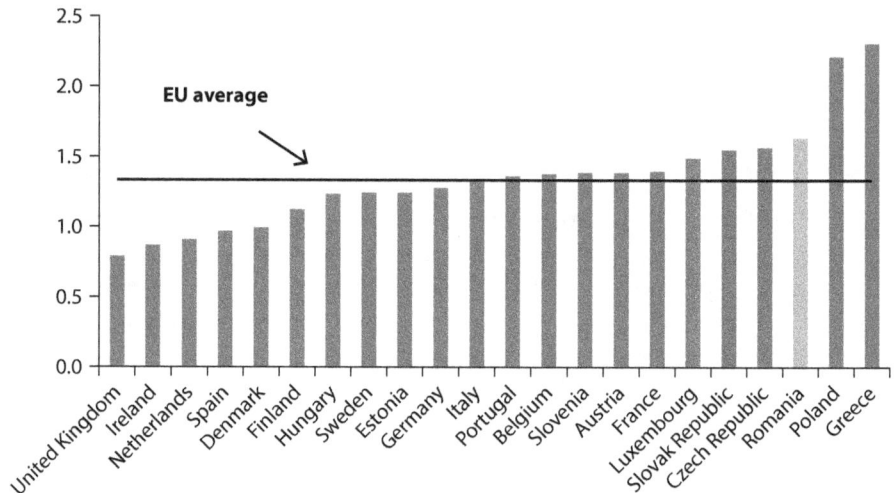

Source: World Bank 2013b.

Note: The vertical axis indicates ranking from 0 (least restrictive) to 6 (most restrictive).

State participation in a significant share of the economy can have detrimental effects on the market and crowd out private investment. The PMR indicator for state control indicates that Romania is the fourth most restrictive of 22 EU countries, surpassed only by Greece, Portugal and Poland.[b] State-operated enterprises (SOEs) produce 11.5 percent of value added in the economy (World Bank 2013). The state controls at least one company in 16 economic sectors, including upstream sectors like gas, electricity, telecommunications, railways, roads, and water. In 2010, the operating income of the 10 largest SOEs represented 4.6 percent of GDP.[c] While SOE presence in the network industries is not unusual in many EU economies, the government's share in the largest enterprise in many network industries is significantly higher than the EU average, especially for gas production and transmission, airline transportation, and telecommunications (figures B1.1.2 and B1.1.3).

box continues next page

Box 1.1 Restrictiveness of Product Market Regulations in Romania *(continued)*

Figure B1.1.2 PMR for State Control of Economic Activity, EU Countries

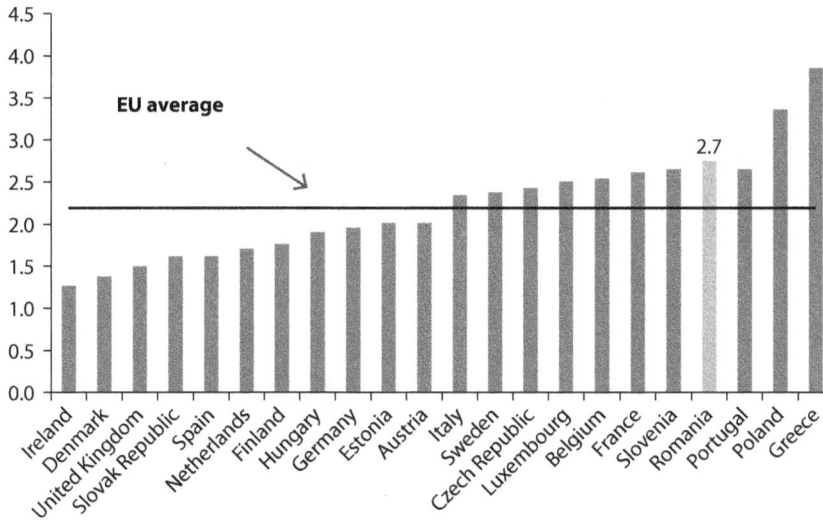

Source: World Bank 2013b.

Note: Vertical axis goes from 0 (least restrictive) to 6 (most restrictive).

Figure B1.1.3 PMR for Government Involvement in Infrastructure, EU Countries

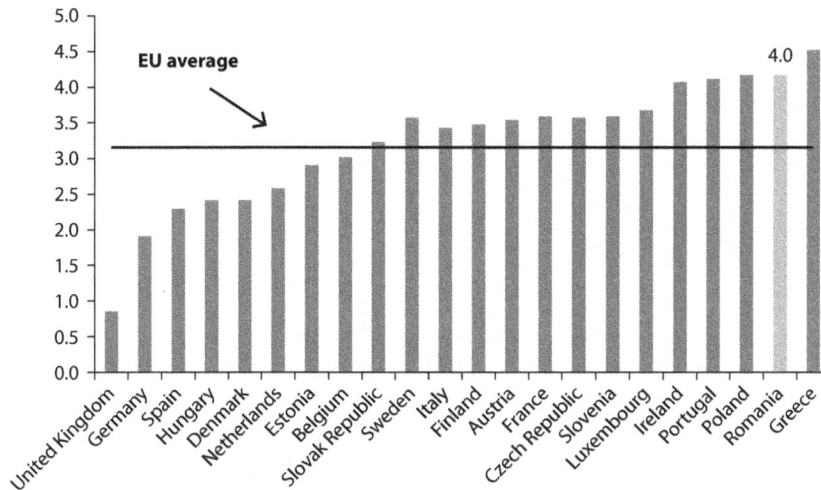

Source: World Bank 2013b.

Note: Vertical axis goes from 0 (least restrictive) to 6 (most restrictive).

Barriers to FDI are higher in Romania than the EU average (figure B1.1.4). The same is true for barriers to FDI (figure B1.1.5).[d] Copaciu (2011, cited in World Bank 2013a) found that FDI is positively related to the quality of competition policy legislation. In the energy sector, the Romania Fiscal Council (2011, cited in World Bank 2013a) has underscored the importance of procom-

box continues next page

Box 1.1 Restrictiveness of Product Market Regulations in Romania *(continued)*

petitive regulations that send the right investment signals and are evenly applied to all companies in a given sector. Fair competition practices and the independence of regulators also help to attract investment. FDI in Romania from EU partners represented between 6 percent and 9 percent of GDP each year between 2004 and 2008. Even so, among the EU-10 countries, Romania continues to have the lowest per capita inward FDI (World Bank 2013).

Figure B1.1.4 PMR for Barriers to Trade and Investment, EU Countries

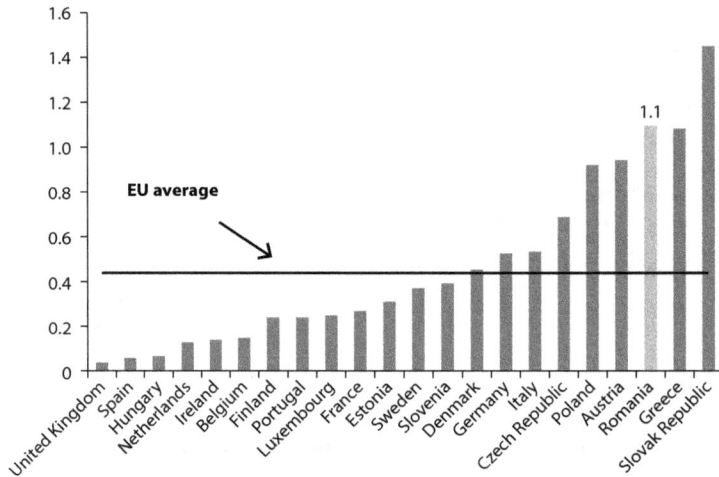

Source: World Bank 2013b.
Note: Vertical axis goes from 0 (least restrictive) to 6 (most restrictive).

Figure B1.1.5 PMR for Barriers to FDI, EU Countries

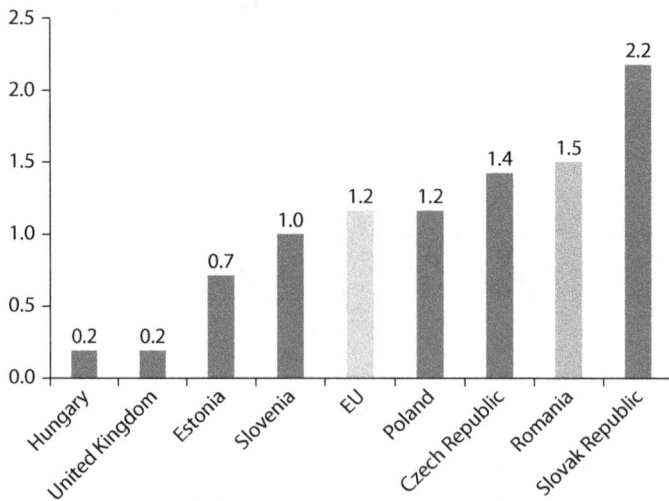

Source: World Bank 2013b.
Note: The vertical axis measures from 0 (least restrictive) to 6 (most restrictive).

box continues next page

Box 1.1 Restrictiveness of Product Market Regulations in Romania *(continued)*

a. The PMR assesses the degree to which policies promote or inhibit market forces in several areas of the product market. The PMR indicators rate the degree to which regulations restrict competition on a scale of 0 (least restrictive) to 6 (most restrictive), both economy-wide and in key sectors of the economy. They measure officially adopted policies, not implementation or enforcement. The PMR covers three main policy areas: state control, barriers to entrepreneurship, and barriers to trade and investment. It also provides sector-specific information on electricity, gas, telecom, post, transport, water, retail distribution, and professional services. It is composed of 18 basic indicators that each capture a specific aspect of the policy environment and that are calculated on the basis of qualitative and quantitative information. The PMR information reflects 2011 data for Romania and 2008 information for all EU comparators (World Bank, 2013).

b. The Product Market Regulation (PMR) indicator for state control of the OECD covers five policy areas: scope of public enterprise, government involvement in network sectors, direct control over business enterprise, price controls, and use of command-and-control regulation.

c. The top 10 network SOEs in 2010 were Electrica Furnizare, Romgaz, Hidroelectrica, Caile Ferate Romane, Translelectrica, Nuclearelectrica, Posta Romana, Transgaz, TAROM, and Electrica Serv. Including Petrom and Romtelecom, which are not majority publicly owned, the operating income to GDP ratio increases to 8 percent.

d. The PMR barriers to trade and investment indicator covers four policy areas: barriers to FDI, tariffs, discriminatory procedures, and regulatory barriers.

Source: World Bank 2013b.

Romania's ability to prosper in the EU's common market requires a stronger competition policy framework. Overall, the Treaty on the Functioning of the European Union ("TFEU" or the "Treaty") covers competition rules applicable to EU member countries, including Romania (Articles 101 to 109).[2] Articles 101 and 102 of the TFEU deal with the anticompetitive business practices that result from coordinated behavior between competitors and from the unilateral conduct of firms with significant market power. Merger regulations provide rules to assess the potential competitive harm of economic concentrations. These regulations cover horizontal, vertical and conglomerate mergers and acquisitions.[3] In this sense, Articles 101 and 102 regulate the conduct of firms, while merger regulations focus on the structure and consolidation of markets. In addition, the European Commission (EC) has the sole responsibility to control any state aid that distorts or threatens to distort competition by favoring certain markets or firms (either private or public) (Articles 107 to 109 TFEU) (figure 1.1).

A comprehensive competition policy framework rests on two complementary pillars: opening markets to competition by addressing sector-specific constraints; and enforcing competition policies (table 1.1). Both pillars rely on an institutional setup that can foster and guarantee healthy market conduct. The independence—that is, autonomy of decisions—of the competition authority and the process of promoting competition rather than consumer protection, seem to drive total factor productivity (TFP) growth. In a study using cross-country evidence, Voigt (2009) estimates that the de facto independence of the competition authority in a developing country can translate, on average, into a 17 percentage point reduction in the TFP gap with the United States.

Figure 1.1 Typology of Competition Rules in the EU

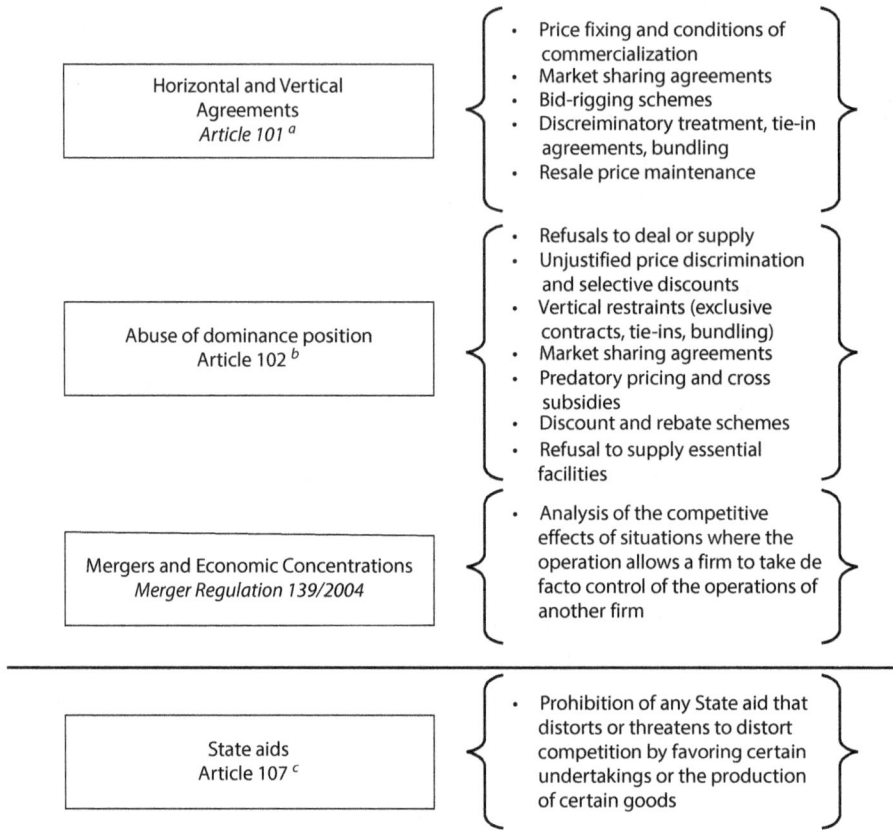

Horizontal and Vertical Agreements Article 101 [a]	• Price fixing and conditions of commercialization • Market sharing agreements • Bid-rigging schemes • Discreiminatory treatment, tie-in agreements, bundling • Resale price maintenance
Abuse of dominance position Article 102 [b]	• Refusals to deal or supply • Unjustified price discrimination and selective discounts • Vertical restraints (exclusive contracts, tie-ins, bundling) • Market sharing agreements • Predatory pricing and cross subsidies • Discount and rebate schemes • Refusal to supply essential facilities
Mergers and Economic Concentrations Merger Regulation 139/2004	• Analysis of the competitive effects of situations where the operation allows a firm to take de facto control of the operations of another firm
State aids Article 107 [c]	• Prohibition of any State aid that distorts or threatens to distort competition by favoring certain undertakings or the production of certain goods

a. Prohibition does not apply to particular agreements (R&D, distribution) that do not distort competition.
b. It requires the existence of a dominant position.
c. Aid can be granted in specific circumstances (e.g., to promote the economic developments of areas where the standard of living is abnormally low).

Table 1.1 A Comprehensive Competition Policy Framework

Opening markets and removing anticompetitive sectoral regulation	Effectively enforcing competition law and rules economy-wide
Remove restrictions to the number of firms, statutory monopolies, or bans toward private investment	Tackle cartel agreements that raise the costs of key inputs and final products
Eliminate controls on prices and other market variables that increase business risk	Prevent anticompetitive mergers
Guarantee a level playing field and nondiscriminatory treatment of certain firms	Strengthen antitrust framework to combat anticompetitive conduct
	Control state aid/incentives to avoid favoritism and ensure competitive neutrality

Source: Kitzmuller and Licetti 2012.

The 2010 functional review of the RCC highlighted the need for a whole-of-government approach to integrate competition principles into Romania's public administration. The review of the RCC was part of a broader strategic and functional assessment of Romania's central public administration by the World Bank on behalf of the Government of Romania.[4] Compared with counterparts in the EU, several areas of competition policy enforcement required improvement, particularly improving cartel enforcement. Few anticompetitive business practice cases were concluded in a timely manner. Workloads focused primarily on merger review procedures with few resources available for conducting advanced economic analyses. Systematic monitoring of state aid rules was key, given widespread state support of SOEs. And there were only a few internal targets to track the performance of the RCC's enforcement and advocacy. On the basis of the recommendations of the functional review, the RCC and the government endorsed a Reform Action Plan (2012) that proposed a three-prong strategy to strengthen Romania's competitive framework:

- The government needs to take practical steps to deepen its commitment to advancing competition in Romania. For this mission, the RCC needs major internal restructuring to move personnel and resources to the frontline of competition enforcement, especially in identifying and breaking up cartels and in addressing the abuse of dominance practices.
- The RCC should sharpen its mission, undertake and publish a coherent strategy backed by results indicators in line with EU comparators, and strengthen the quality control and priorities of its strategic efforts.
- The RCC should strengthen its capacity by promoting program-based budgeting, public accountability, merit-based human resource management, and modern information technology and communication infrastructure.

At the RCC's request, the World Bank initiated a US$2.4 million Reimbursable Advisory Services program with the Romanian government. This program's goal was to implement the Action Plan and to improve the effectiveness of competition policies—among them, enforcement of the competition law and integration of competition principles in sectoral policies. The program provided targeted advice to address challenges in the RCC's core functions: a legal and regulatory framework that governs competition; an operational framework that enables a well-functioning competition agency; enforcement of the competition law and creation of a competition culture through a strong competition-advocacy program (orange-shaded areas in figure 1.2). Competition policy ultimately ensures effective market functioning, while state aid control is particularly important to enhance the effectiveness of public sector spending and to rationalize support measures to SOEs. The RAS took place from June 2012 to May 2015. This report describes the advisory services in each of these core areas, including the challenges, solutions, and actions for each.

Figure 1.2   Implementing the Competition Policy Framework

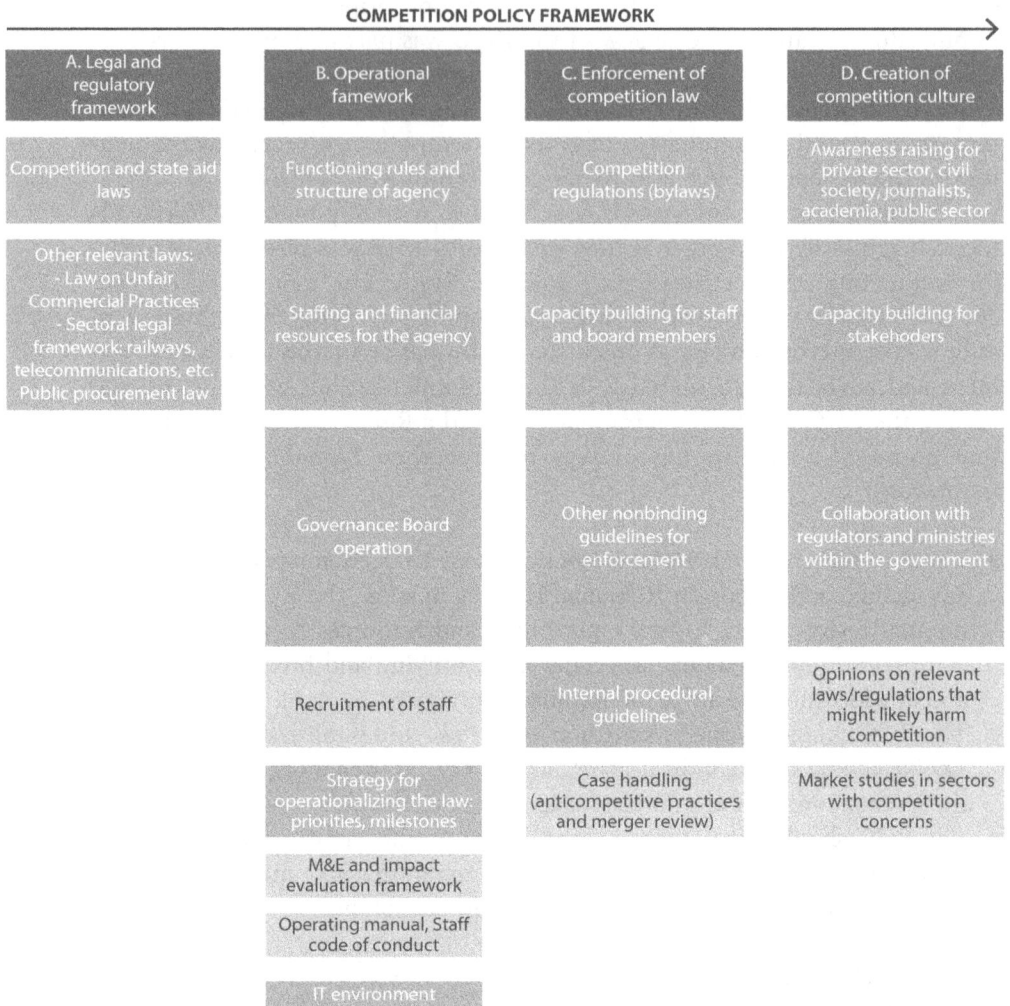

COMPETITION POLICY FRAMEWORK →

A. Legal and regulatory framework	B. Operational famework	C. Enforcement of competition law	D. Creation of competition culture
Competition and state aid laws	Functioning rules and structure of agency	Competition regulations (bylaws)	Awareness raising for private sector, civil society, journalists, academia, public sector
Other relevant laws: - Law on Unfair Commercial Practices - Sectoral legal framework: railways, telecommunications, etc. Public procurement law	Staffing and financial resources for the agency	Capacity building for staff and board members	Capacity building for stakehoders
	Governance: Board operation	Other nonbinding guidelines for enforcement	Collaboration with regulators and ministries within the government
	Recruitment of staff	Internal procedural guidelines	Opinions on relevant laws/regulations that might likely harm competition
	Strategy for operationalizing the law: priorities, milestones	Case handling (anticompetitive practices and merger review)	Market studies in sectors with competition concerns
	M&E and impact evaluation framework		
	Operating manual, Staff code of conduct		
	IT environment		

Source: World Bank, Trade and Competitiveness Global Practice-Competition Policy Team, 2015

Note: Separate agencies are in charge of developing sector-specific regulation in the field of railways services, telecommunications, public procurement, and so on.

Notes

1. Much of this growth was driven by a reallocation of labor from less productive sectors like agriculture, to more productive sectors like services and construction.
2. Official Journal C 83 of March 30, 2010.
3. Horizontal mergers are those that involve firms actually or potentially competing in the same market, vertical mergers are those between firms present at different levels of the supply chain, and conglomerate mergers are those between noncompeting firms and in different supply chains.
4. As laid out in the June 2009 Memorandum of Understanding between the World Bank and the Government of Romania [GoR].

CHAPTER 2

Legal and Regulatory Framework Governing Market Competition

Introduction

While markets are often robust, some market participants occasionally act deliberately to thwart competitive forces. They might agree with rival firms to compete less aggressively. They might prevent new entry, force rivals from the market, or otherwise diminish competition. Or, they might merge to unify competitors or vertically related firms into single economic units that impede effective competition in the market. Competition law prevents such activities from disrupting competition and harming consumer welfare.

A better alignment of the Romania Competition Council (RCC)'s legal and policy framework, mission, and institutional capacity was one of the key strategic areas identified to sharpen its effectiveness in promoting competitive market conditions. To achieve this goal, reimbursable technical assistance aimed to make the RCC more agile and bring the RCC's legal framework in line with EU regulations. Further aligning Romania's competition policy framework with the European Union (EU)'s is not only a legal obligation—it is an opportunity for this country to further benefit from economic integration with the European internal market.

To achieve these goals, the advisory services program supported a review of Romania's legal framework for competition, including the competition law, the state aid procedural rules and the law on unfair commercial practices.

The Romanian Competition Law

An effective competition policy framework depends on the quality of the competition law and the ability to implement it. Typically, competition law aims at promoting market efficiency, low prices, and high-quality goods and services. The objective is to encourage open markets that allow new businesses to enter and compete on equal footing with competitors, thus encouraging efficiency and innovation. Competition laws cover business practices that restrict, distort, or prevent competition among firms. Restricted competition can stem from anticompetitive agreements among competitors or from a firm's dominant position in a market. In addition, competition laws contain provisions on merger control to prevent harmful concerted practices that may result from certain economic concentrations. The World Bank Group team identified key elements that appear to limit both the quality of the Romanian Competition Law and the ability of the RCC to implement it.[1]

Challenges

While the current version of the Romania Competition Law[2] is broadly in line with the EU rules, it does not allow the RCC to focus on public interest cases and policies coherent with the agency priorities, thus wasting time and resources on nonpriority cases. Within the broad scope of functions and tasks assigned to competition agencies, priorities become essential. Unlike sector regulators, which have a clearly defined scope of intervention, competition agencies have to assess the behavior of economic agents across many sectors. Setting priorities between casework and noncasework is crucial for an agency to operate effectively with increasing caseloads and limited resources. An effective competition law should enable the RCC to set priorities based on the expected effects of its actions.

Finding the correct balance between transparency, procedural fairness and the rights of the defense on the one hand, and the need to proceed efficiently with decisions on complex cases within reasonable deadlines on the other, presents a constant challenge to competition authorities. On any given case, many procedural decisions that need to be taken—either internally, by the President of the RCC, or externally, by the Bucharest Court of Appeals—can hinder efficiency and lead to unnecessary delays.

The Romania Competition Law unduly burdens the private sector through redundant or unnecessary procedures, increasing the cost of doing business in Romania. For example, a presumption of dominance set at 40 percent of market share and burdensome merger review procedures—including low notification thresholds, onerous information requests and long review periods—limits the ability of Romanian companies to compete. Moreover, the position and liability of the private sector in certain antitrust cases need to be considered in relation to the current scope of sanctions, particularly the elimination of (high) minimum fines as well as the criminal enforceability of antitrust violations where the conditions and criteria for sanctioning individuals for antitrust crimes remain unclear.

Solutions

The World Bank's analysis identified provisions of the competition law that limit the ability of the RCC to prioritize actions. To enhance the RCC's efficiency, its ability to prioritize competition complaints needs to be revised. Additionally, when complaints are rejected, complainants still have a right to be heard. This represents a superfluous administrative burden for the RCC that goes beyond international standards for due process and can be eliminated. Furthermore, after a thorough investigation, cases that still reveal no infringement of competition rules should be quickly closed.

In line with EU practice, the World Bank Group team proposed to clarify and limit the role of the president in several ways. First, some of its current functions should be reshuffled to an independent "hearing officer." This hearing officer would be in charge of a number of procedural concerns, including matters of confidentiality and legal privilege. Second, some of his or her other current functions (for example, assigning case handlers) should be assigned to a neutral registrar.

Further amendments to the Romania Competition Law include the following:

- Empowering the RCC to focus on cases and mergers that are coherent with its priorities and that have a greater impact on competition law and develop fast-track procedures for less important mergers
- Enhancing procedural effectiveness through the de-judicialization of competition enforcement
- Reducing unnecessary burdens on the private sector by clarifying the obligation to consult with the Supreme Council of National Defense, better articulating the Romanian Competition Law (RCL) with the Treaty on the Functioning of the European Union (TFEU), and deleting the 40 percent threshold for the presumption of dominance; improving the RCC's enforcement and sanctioning powers by replacing "total turnover" with "affected turnover" and by encouraging the prosecutor's office to criminally prosecute cartels
- Removing the government's ability to impose price controls.

Results

A new draft competition law, under preparation, is expected to incorporate several RAS recommendations:

- Removing merger notification thresholds from its text and including them in merger regulations that can be regularly updated without cumbersome legislative procedures
- Eliminating the threshold for a presumption of dominance
- Providing greater legal certainty by clarifying deadlines and prescription-term provisions
- Removing provisions governing price controls
- Limiting the opportunity to challenge the RCC's final decisions before the Court of Appeal on grounds of access to file and confidentiality
- Creating the position of independent procedural officer, separate from the enforcement teams within the RCC, specializing in access to file, confidentiality, and other procedural matters
- Clarifying provisions on legal privilege and on fining rules (for example, introducing the possibility of rewarding whistleblowers with an amount up to 1 percent of the fine imposed by the RCC; establishing a legal deadline for parties to propose commitments that eliminate the cause of the infringement and to apply for a fine reduction).

The State Aid Law

State aid can distort competitive market conditions by providing undue advantages to some firms over others. Article 107(1) TFEU defines state aid as "any aid granted by a Member State or through State resources in any form whatsoever which distorts or threatens to distort competition by favoring certain undertakings or the production of certain foods". State aid alters the reward-sanctions mechanisms in a competitive market, effectively introducing barriers to trade that have been abolished in the EU, and may represent an unnecessary cost for the public and, ultimately, taxpayers. However, well-targeted state aid can address market failures and support economic policy objectives. For example, it can reduce regional disparities, promote research and development and stimulate initiatives to improve environmental standards. For this reason, the TFEU provides that some state aid might be compatible (Article 107(2) TFEU) or might be declared compatible with the internal market by the Commission (Article 107(3) TFEU), depending on whether it has positive effects.[3]

In Romania, the share of state aid in gross domestic product (GDP) rose from 0.16 percent in 2010 to 0.45 percent in 2012. The increase came from providing state aid for environmental protection and energy production from renewable sources and cogenerating processes. During the same period, the share of state aid awarded for sectoral objectives fell from 31 percent to around 7 percent, a result of terminating state aid for restructuring and closing coal mines.[4] In 2013, horizontal aid represented 91 percent of total aid, while sectoral aid was only 5 percent of the total aid granted in the same year.[5] These trends are consistent with EU recommendations that promote state aid toward horizontal objectives, given their less harmful effects on the competitive environment.

As in the other EU Member States, state aid control rules apply to aid provided to both private firms and state-operated enterprises (SOEs). Controlling how state aid is granted is particularly relevant in the Romanian market, which still exhibits a significant SOE presence (about 645 at the end of 2012). Most harmful to the economy are the SOEs that either produce more than half of their sector's output (such as gas and electricity) or heavily influence it (telecoms, railroads, road-building storage, mining, and quarrying). The government has already begun a reform program, which included (i) ending subsidies for all SOEs without demonstrable social value; (ii) privatizing SOEs in chemicals, freight transport, and energy; and (iii) professionalizing the management of SOEs that remain in state hands (World Bank 2013b). In this context, state aid rules ensure that the awarding of economic advantages to SOEs and other privileged firms that directly compete with private firms in the market do not distort competition conditions.

The European Commission has exclusive competence to assess the compatibility of a proposed measure with the internal market, the so-called "balancing test" in which the common interest is assessed on the basis of the effects of the aid on competition and trade (this test includes an economic evaluation of the aid). However, the Commission and member states share the responsibility for ensuring that EU state aid procedures work. The application of EU state aid rules within the different member states, including Romania, requires the implementation of certain internal procedural rules. EU law only requires that these internal rules ensure the good functioning of the EU state aid system.

Challenges

Romania should strengthen its legal framework for state aid[6] and further align it with the latest EU framework ("State Aid Modernization")[7] in a way that effectively tackles the risks related to increased administrative discretion and market distortions that stem from the RCC's unclear relationship with state aid–granting authorities and courts (in case unlawful state aid needs to be recovered). This is essential for the RCC to monitor the effects of state aid on the Romanian economy, especially because the application of EU state aid rules requires implementing certain internal procedural rules. The Romanian regulatory framework is not fully fledged in the areas of (i) sanctioning powers in case aid is granted illegally and (ii) reviewing regulations on block exemptions of state aid[8] and possibly de minimis aid[9] in accordance with EU law and (iii) clarifying the position of national courts in state aid cases. In addition, ex ante cost-benefit analysis of aid and ex post monitoring of aid effects would require further development. Further recommendations were provided on a draft Emergency Ordinance in order to avoid conflicts with EU law—in particular, the Ordinance suggests that the draft law omits articles that repeat wholly or partially provisions and definitions of EU law that are directly applicable in Romania.

Solutions

To tackle these outstanding issues, the proposed changes to Romania's state aid law aim to bring the regulatory framework closer to EU rules. This can be done through clarifying the obligations of granting authorities; detailing the obligations imposed on beneficiaries of state aid; clarifying procedural rules that are applicable to block-exempted state aid; further regulating the recovery process related to unlawful aid; advocating the role of national courts in state aid cases; ensuring transparency toward companies entrusted with delivering public services (so-called "services of general economic interest"—SGEIs), irrespective of whether these companies are publicly or privately owned. Also recommended are raising awareness and devoting sufficient resources of the RCC to state aid matters.

Results

Romania enacted the Emergency Ordinance 77/2014 on state aid national-level procedures that builds on the above RAS recommendations. The Ordinance aims to clarify issues related to state aid notification, obligations of state aid granting authorities, the role of national courts, and de minims aid.

Moving Forward

The RCC indicated that further support from the World Bank to reduce state aid distortions would be welcome. Several areas would require further action by the RCC. These relate to assessing the impact of strategic state aid schemes, automating state aid data collection to increase transparency on amounts granted and objectives pursued, and helping with the process of reporting to the EU Commission, while further strengthening state aid awareness among local and national granting authorities.

The Unfair Competition Law

In addition to the mandate to protect free competition in Romania, the RCC is in charge of applying the Unfair Competition Law (UCL).[10] This law seeks to punish unfair commercial practices that, rather than affecting the market as a whole, affect the position of individual competitors and their spheres of interest. Unfair commercial practices include, for instance, betraying business secrets or violating the reputation of a business.[11]

Challenges

An effective regulatory framework for unfair commercial practices must be consistent with procedures to fight antitrust violations under the Romanian Competition Law. In addition to loopholes[12] in the UCL and overlaps with the RCL, the effectiveness of the UCL has been hampered by the RCC's inability to prioritize unfair competition cases and make clear distinctions between the RCL and the UCL (for example, to distinguish unfair prices from predatory pricing).

Solutions

The advisory services program recommends establishing a "de minimis test," which identifies an infringement as an act that prevents achievement of the law's objectives. Also recommended is an "opportunity test," where the RCC becomes involved only if the public interest or market structure are affected.

Results

The recommendations were adopted in a government ordinance in August 2014. Government Ordinance 12/2014, modifying Law 11/1990 on fighting unfair competition, protects consumers, competitors and other market participants in a way that complements and expands the scope of other laws, such as the RCL or the Consumer Protection Law.[13] Ordinance 12/2014 incorporates core RAS recommendations, including an "opportunity test" to trigger RCC's competence (that is, public interest or the market structure must be affected) and a general unfair competition law catch-all clause.[14] Furthermore, the Ordinance offers a clearer definition of the purpose of the law and aligns the terminology used with that of EU law. In addition to Ordinance 12/2014, the RCC enacted a Procedural

Regulation on November 24, 2014, which clarifies the opportunity test and issues of capacity to submit complaints with the RCC.[15]

Moving Forward

As a medium-term strategy, the RCC intends to undertake an ex post analysis of the new unfair competition policy with the assistance of the World Bank.

Sector-Specific Legal Framework Governing Competition: The Railways Legislation Package

Romania's railways went through radical reforms during the early transition years, but few changes have occurred since.[16] Railways, a key input sector, have great potential for advancing economic growth, consumer benefits, social development, and environmental protection. To realize this potential requires fully developing the railway infrastructure, opening railway markets to competition, and improving the interoperability and safety of national networks in line with EU legislation. In 1998, Romania separated the national rail operator into different companies, following a "vertical separation" model, and introduced competition through open access to the infrastructure (OECD 2013). A recurrent recipient of state aid, the sector had been dominated by SOEs[17] and their subsidiaries. But all new private freight operators entered the sector after 1998, eroding the market share of the main operator, CFR Marfă.

For the EU, liberalizing railways is critical for its internal market. The EU "liberalization packages" have already been implemented in Romania, and one Recast Directive must be implemented by June 16, 2015.[18]

Challenges

Romania must reform its railway legislation to revitalize the sector and better integrate Romanian and EU markets.[19] These reforms would strengthen the regulatory framework of railways and separate accounting between rail infrastructure and rail services. The Railways Supervisory Council (RSC) became part of the RCC in 2011 to oversee the sector's functioning and market conditions. But railway legislation still lacked clarity and guidance on the scope of the powers and competences of the RSC, on the RSC's access charges for rail tracks and related services and on the compensation of public service contracts for passenger rail services.

Solutions

The World Bank Group extensively reviewed Romania railway's legal and regulatory framework. The aim was to boost competition, strengthen the RSC's powers, develop the internal market for rail transport, and improve the competitiveness of the railway sector. The World Bank team recommended adopting six key elements set forth in the EU Railways "Recast Directive": clarify the powers and competences of the RSC, define the role of the infrastructure manager, increase transparency for entering the railway market, define the "financial structure" of the railways sector, clarify infrastructure charging rules, and provide guidance to determine compensation for public service contracts.

Results

The RSC and the Ministry of Justice endorsed a draft law initiated by the Ministry of Transport that will implement the EU Recast Directive (the law establishing the single European railway space on Romanian territory).

Telecommunications: Broadband Infrastructure

Challenges

High-speed broadband is important for the competitiveness of businesses in the Romanian market.[20] A lack of clear rules on public support for network deployment may hold back the connectivity and coverage for businesses in isolated areas and increase the risk of administrative discretion and market distortions. Broadband infrastructure networks, strongly interconnected with other sectors of the economy, are a source of essential inputs with spillovers across the economy. Greater penetration of high-speed broadband should spur innovation, more affordable services, and pro-competitive investments that ultimately raise economic growth and improve daily life for both citizens and businesses. To meet this challenge, private investment needs to be supplemented by public financing, which could raise concerns of unfairness among firms, wrong allocation of support between black-and-white areas, and crowding-out of private investment.[21]

Solutions

The World Bank supports developing internal guidance to assess public support for developing broadband network infrastructure. These guidelines provide a framework to analyze state aid measures that should enable funding entities to achieve a faster rate of broadband coverage and penetration while maintaining a level-playing field between operators. Another solution is to enhance the collaboration between the RCC and ANCOM, the telecom regulator. To achieve this goal, it is recommended that public support for broadband infrastructure not undermine private incentives to invest and not focus on black areas, that is, areas where market operators have already invested or would normally choose to invest. Also recommended are ensuring open access to broadband infrastructure to foster downstream competition and relieving the administrative burden of state aid notification by using alternative means of support that do not fall under state aid rules. Examples include services of general economic interest, noncommercial operations that can be used at no cost, and public–private partnerships.

Results

The RCC approved guidelines to assess public support for deploying broadband network infrastructure in 2014.

Electronic Communications

Challenges

Electronic communications are fast evolving toward high-speed data transfers to meet the growing demand for mobile data services and in mobile infrastructure. Romania's telecommunications regulatory framework is aligned to that of the EU, and competition in this market is fierce. But several aspects of the framework require greater clarification. For example, competition conditions in the sector must be addressed, business costs contained, and the inefficient use of RCC resources to understand the effects of network sharing agreements in wireless broadband markets should be improved. Special attention should be paid to infrastructure-sharing agreements among operators because these are relevant for upgrading networks.[22]

Romania needs to strengthen its ability to assess network-sharing agreements. Such agreements may enhance efficiency and improve coverage and quality of service for consumers and businesses. They limit duplication and gear investments toward underserved areas. They also improve broadband coverage and speeds in high-demand areas, while encouraging companies to focus on innovation. But the integration between mobile network operators can vary greatly, and competition issues may arise if network sharing creates a dominant position in the market.

Solutions

The World Bank Group helped the RCC and the telecom regulator develop guidelines that define how competition rules are applied to network-sharing agreements. The guidelines analyze the implications of infrastructure-sharing agreements. Passive infrastructure-sharing agreements raise fewer competition concerns than active sharing because they do not require sharing network elements, nor result in the high commonality of costs, nor involve significant information and forecasting exchanges between competitors. The degree of cooperation increases in active infrastructure agreements, which raises the risk of collusion. Other factors in assessing the competition risks of network sharing include the geographic scope of the agreement, the market power of the operators, the duration of the agreement and the parties' commercial independence.

Results

In 2014, the RCC published Guidelines on network-sharing agreements building on the RAS results and offering a framework for the assessment of both passive and active sharing of infrastructure.

Competitive Processes Associated with Public Procurement

Challenges

Embedding competition principles in public procurement policy ensures low prices and higher-quality goods and services.[23] Collaboration with the Public

Procurement Agency (ANRMAP)[24] can be useful for the RCC to assess patterns in procurement processes and identify indications of potential anticompetitive practices in public procurement. The role of the RCC in this is twofold: ex ante the RCC can act to make bidding processes more competitive to reduce the risk of collusion in the first place; and ex post should prosecute bid-rigging cartels to discourage bidders from entering collusive agreements. On the former, there was a gap regarding clear guidance to public procurement officials on principles for the design of pro-competitive public tenders.

Solutions

The Word Bank Group advised on how to design more competitive public tenders. The guidelines propose questions that allow public officials to apply a competition filter when designing public tenders—in four steps:

- How to select the most pro-competitive procurement procedure? Contracting authorities should understand that the procedure they choose will determine the competition conditions of the tender. They should gather information regarding market conditions and choose the procedure that best fits the market. They should minimize the anticompetitive impacts generated by a procedure and publish a participation notice that announces the tender.
- How to design the terms of the tender to favor competition? The tender should prevent discrimination against bidders.
- How to avoid anticompetitive decisions during the tendering process? The contracting agency should provide equal access to information, be able to remedy errors and make calls for tenders public and transparent.

How to avoid anticompetitive decisions after the tendering process? Tools to avoid them include monitoring subcontracting arrangements and strictly limiting modifications to the provision of complementary services.

Notes

1. Deliverable 1.1.3: Recommendations to strengthen the Romanian Competition Law, February 2014.
2. Competition Law no. 21/1996, and subsequent amendments.
3. Deliverable 1.1.2: Analysis and Review of the State Aid Legal and Regulatory Framework, April 2013.
4. Romanian Competition Council: http://www.stateaid.ro/?pag=139&limba=en#ajutor-destat.
5. http://www.ajutordestat.ro/?pag=139&limba=ro#ajutordestat.
6. The national procedures in the field of state aid, as developed by the Emergency Ordinance Decree no.117/2006 (the "Emergency Ordinance" or "Ordinance"), in conjunction with the Regulation on the procedures to monitor State aid (the "Monitoring Regulation"), establish a series of rules which is sufficient to ensure that Romania complies with its main responsibilities in State aid matters.

7. http://ec.europa.eu/competition/state_aid/modernisation/index_en.html

8. See endnote 1 in executive summary.

9. See endnote 1 in executive summary.

10. The Romanian law against unfair competition has no complete codification of the relevant aspects of unfair competition. There are different Sources: Law No. 11 of January 29, 1991, on the repression of unfair competition amended in 2003; Law No. 504/2002–Audiovisual Law; Law No. 148/2000 on advertising; Law No. 158/2008 on misleading advertising and comparative advertising, implementing Directive 2006/114/EC; and Law No. 363/2007 on combating improper practices of traders in their relations with consumers, implementing the Directive 2005/29/EC concerning unfair business-to-consumer commercial practices.

11. Deliverable 1.1.1: Report on Recommendations to Amend the Unfair Competition law, January 2013.

12. Examples include allocation of competences, alternative dispute settlements, and the RCC's use of sensitive information.

13. Core RAS recommendations included the need to establish first a "de minimis test," that is, infringement only occurs if the action proves relevant to achieving the law's objectives; and second, an "opportunity test," that is, public interest or the market structure should be affected, be verified in order to trigger the competence of the RCC.

14. Another core RAS recommendation included the need to establish first, a "de minimis test," that is, infringement only occurs if the action proves relevant to achieving the objectives of the law.

15. Implemented by the Order no. 561 of November 24, 2014, published in Official Gazette No. 918 dated December 17, 2014.

16. Deliverable 1.1.4, 1.3.9. a and b: Review of the legal and regulatory framework governing market competition of the railways legislation package, June 2014.

17. The National Railway (Infrastructure) Company (CFR SA), the National Railway (Passenger) Company (CFR Călători), and the National Railway (Freight) Company (CFR Marfă).

18. The Recast Directive, which consolidates several former Directives into one single document, and aims to (i) enhance competition, namely by increasing transparency of market access conditions, and improve access to rail-related services, (ii) foster investment in railway infrastructure, and (iii) create a stricter regulatory oversight where the powers of the regulator are strengthened. The first railways liberalization legislation dates from the 1990s: Directive 91/440/EEC on the development of the community's railways, Directive 95/18/EC on the licensing of Railway Undertakings and Directive 95/19/EC on allocation of railway infrastructure capacity, and the charging of infrastructure fees and Directive 96/48/EC of July 23, 1996, on the interoperability of the trans-European high-speed rail system. This first set of Directives was followed by three Packages and a Recast Directive, which consolidates the different pieces of legislation into one single document: (First Package): Directive 2001/12/EC amending Council Directive 91/440/EEC on the development of the Community's railways, Directive 2001/13/EC amending Council Directive 95/18/EC on the licensing of railway undertakings and Directive 2001/14/EC on the allocation of railway infrastructure capacity, and the levying of charges for the use of railway infrastructure and safety certification; (Second Package): Directive 2004/49/EC on safety on the

Community's railways, Directive 2004/50/EC on the interoperability of the trans-European high-speed rail system and the trans-European conventional rail system, Directive 2004/51/EC amending Council Directive 91/440/EEC on the development of the Community's railways, and Regulation 881/2004 establishing a European Railway Agency; (Third Package): Directive 2007/58/EC amending Council Directive 91/440/EEC on the development of the Community's railways and Directive 2001/14/EC on the allocation of railway infrastructure capacity and the levying of charges for the use of railway infrastructure, Directive 2007/59/EC on the certification of train drivers operating locomotives and trains on the railway system in the Community, Regulation (EC) 1371/2007 on rail passengers' rights and obligations and Directive 2008/57/EC of June 17, 2008 on railway interoperability; (Recast Directive): Directive 2012/34/EU establishing a single European railway area and Directive 2012/34, which Romania had to implement by June 16, 2015.

19. Government Ordinance No. 89/2003.

20. Deliverable 1.3.3: Internal guidance on the assessment of public support for broadband networks infrastructure deployment, June 2014.

21. See EU Guidelines for the application of state aid rules in relation to the rapid deployment of broadband networks, OJ C25, January 26, 2013.

22. Deliverable 1.3.8: Comments addressed to guidelines on competition assessment in electronic communications, June 2014.

23. Deliverable 1.3.7: Quick Guidelines on Public Procurement, September 2013.

24. The Public Procurement Agency (ANRMAP) is the main agency ensuring the regulatory supervision of the public procurement system in Romania. It is important to highlight that several institutions/stakeholders have roles and responsibilities in the field of public procurement. However, a distinction should be made between institutions that have competencies exclusively in the public procurement field (that is, ANRMAP, Unit for Coordinating and Verifying Public Procurement (Ministry of Public Finances)(UCVAP), and National Council for Solving Complaints [CNSC]) and those that intervene in regulating/controlling/sanctioning/supporting different aspects of the public procurement system (that is, the National Management Centre for the Informational Society [CNMSI], the Competition Council, the Managing Authorities (MAs), the Authority for Certifications and Payments(ACP), the Audit Authority, the Department for Fight against Fraud (DLAF), and the judiciary system).

CHAPTER 3

Operational Framework

Introduction

The Romania Competition Council (RCC) is an autonomous competition agency. An autonomous agency is less vulnerable to lobbying from interest groups, which is especially important for agencies directly responsible for regulating the practices of businesses. An autonomous agency that does not change direction or leadership with every new election will be more consistent and predictable, and its decision making will be less political and more technical. Reducing regulatory uncertainty allows businesses to manage risk. A consistent agency is also more likely to stay focused on the long-term goal of creating a competitive market and less likely to focus on short-term political agendas.[1]

The RCC, with technical assistance from the World Bank Group, has begun to reorganize its functional rules and structure. To do so, it followed an enterprise architecture methodology. The intent was to determine how it could best improve its agility, efficiency, effectiveness, and durability.

The enterprise architecture comprises business, technology, and solutions. The business architecture is the blueprint for systematically defining the current (baseline) and desired (target) organization in business terms, including strategy, functions, information flows, systems and capabilities. The technology architecture defines the technology to enable the business architecture. The solution architecture aligns the business and technology architectures into an implementation plan, known as the migration plan.

In its assessment of the RCC's business architecture, the World Bank identified 39 functional weaknesses. They fall into four categories: capabilities of staffing, rules and structure; visibility and impact in operationalizing the competition law; governance and board operation; and the information technology environment.

Rules, Structure, Staffing, and Strategy

The RCC is a multipurpose competition agency. Competition agencies have functions beyond simply enforcing competition laws, including consumer protection, public procurement, state aid, unfair trading, sector regulation, internal market, assistance to the historically disadvantaged, and SME promotion. The agency's design should reflect its different functions to realize synergies between them and to guarantee a predictable and accountable decision-making process, which is separate from the investigative functions. Therefore, the RAS made recommendations based on key principles for effective competition agencies, with a focus on strategy, and key mandated and enabling functions (figure 3.1).

Challenges

RCC's business architecture has developed organically over the past 15 years. It is characterized by limited internal and external transparency, reduced operational effectiveness, complex organizational processes, a lack of alignment of the staff's roles with institutional objectives, inefficient bundling of investigative and adjudicative functions, and the absence of clear rules for accountability.

The RCC's visibility to the general public and business community is low. For example, the RCC has conducted advocacy cases that removed anticompetitive regulation to the public's benefit, but such success stories normally are not publicized, missing an opportunity to raise awareness of its work.

Solutions

The World Bank Group identified opportunities to increase productivity and effectiveness by aligning RCC processes with EU standards. These opportunities for the RCC include improving internal and external transparency, enhancing operational effectiveness through simplified organizational processes, aligning the roles of staff with institutional objectives, separating investigative from adjudicative functions, providing clear rules for accountability, and pushing responsibilities to the lowest operational level.

Figure 3.1 RCC Activities

There are also other opportunities to strengthen capabilities. They include standardizing processes and procedures and adopting guidelines[2]; distributing workloads according to predetermined criteria; upgrading the registry function; simplifying fast-track procedures for mergers; systematizing deadlines for case analysis and investigations based on EU practices; standardizing forms and checklists for case reviews and case management; setting a dedicated strategic performance management function under the President and Board; and aligning human resources, financial management, and administrative processes with institutional objectives. These changes must be reflected in the RCC's incentive structure and administrative policies and processes.

The RCC should make its advisory processes public and promote them openly, especially for state aid and competition-related regulation. Board decisions to open official antitrust investigations should be published and released to the press. This would demonstrate the potential impact of the investigated practices on consumers and market players. Interested third parties would be encouraged to present observations. Advisory processes on state aid measures should be made public and the impact of such measures on public budgets and the markets should be explained. As a result of such efforts, visibility would improve and lead to the unsolicited participation of market players in the RCC's enforcement activities. Overall, the proposed reforms would strengthen stakeholder awareness of competition laws and policies.

A new strategy, advocacy, and communication unit should be set up to support the RCC's board in formulating its annual strategy. This unit would include analysts, media specialists and competition policy specialists. The strategy will be measured by objectives and key performance indicators, with mechanisms to obtain internal and external feedback, reflected in quarterly reports. These strategic reforms will raise the RCC's visibility as a forum to shape competition in Romania.

Finally, a new business strategy of the RCC needs to be developed to set objectives, prioritize actions and establish performance metrics. This will also help increase accountability. An initial set of business goals, objectives, and metrics were proposed by the World Bank for further development by the RCC, as presented succinctly in table 3.1.

Governance and Board Operations

Challenges

The President, as the Chairman of the Board, is responsible for the functioning of Board and the proper execution of the RCC's overall work. Legally representing the RCC and accountable for all public communication, the President is responsible for direction and overall strategic plan and performance monitoring. He calls for Board meetings, sets the Board's agenda and directs the Board's work. There is no separation between the functions of the President and the execution of the RCC strategy, which also requires a person to direct the operational units and verify their work. The person appointed to this position would report to the President but be accountable to the entire Board.

Building Landmarks, Smoothing Out Markets • http://dx.doi.org/10.1596/978-1-4648-0620-9

Table 3.1 Romania Competition Council (RCC) Strategy and Key Metrics

Goals	Objectives	Key metrics
	Optimize merger processes	
Increase competition across key economic sectors	1. Increase merger notification thresholds 2. Adopt guidelines on the application of the Significant Impediment of Effective Competition 3. Publish notice related to the notification 4. Introduce time-limits in working days 5. Introduce suspension and extension rules 6. Introduce market testing of commitments 7. Introduce "Fast-Track" Procedure for simplified mergers 8. Confidentiality of information aligned to EU Principles	1. Average duration of simplified merger procedure 2. Percentage of pre-notification meetings which successfully settled jurisdictional issues 3. Percentage of unsolicited participation of market players in the RCC merger review 4. Percentage of cases involving the Chief Economist 5. Percentage of notices published related to the concentration
	Enhance competition advocacy	
Create and maintain independence from the government Introduce pro-competition public policies at the sector level	1. Develop a process for carrying out and implementing market studies 2. Align market studies to business strategy and priorities 3. Develop a stakeholder engagement strategy defining when and how to engage stakeholders 4. Identify opportunities for joint market studies with sectoral regulators and public authorities 5. Measure impact of RCC RIA opinion on government proposed/existing regulations 6. Improve regulatory framework to enhance competition 7. Promote active market player participation 8. Engage policy makers to increase exposure of competition issues and link specific recommended changes to policy and/or regulations 9. RCC's points of view/opinions should be more binding	1. Number of new laws/regulations/amendments drafted or contributed to drafting 2. Number of anticompetitive regulations recommended to be changed 3. Number of recommended anticompetitive regulations removed/liminated or minimized 4. Number of instances where government parliament and senate recalls RCC recommendations 5. Number of times an RCC recommendations has been recalled by stakeholders 6. Number of Protocols with regulatory agencies drafted 7. Percentage of non-confidential notice related to RCC review process published 8. Media coverage reported to authorities
	Enhance anti-trust measures	
Align and implement RCC processes to EU practices and law Increase transparency and accountability inside and outside the RCC	1. Increase detection of cartels 2. Monitor competition in regulated markets 3. Increase deterrence effect to anticompetitive behavior 4. Confidentiality of information aligned with EU principles 5. Establish guidelines for leniency and application of cease and desist commitments 6. Eliminate fixed time-tables in preliminary review 7. Enhance economic/econometric analysis and improve visibility 8. Individualize fines, clarify standards for evaluation of mitigation and aggravating factors and application of fine reductions	1. Percentage of cartel cases and exclusionary abusive practices 2. Percentage of leniency application for cartels 3. Percentage of hard-core cartel cases dealt by the Cartel Unit 4. Percentage of ex officio cases opened on key economic sectors 5. Average duration of case 6. Percentage of complaints rejected for reasons of lack of public interest 7. Percentage of complaint and percentage of ex officio cases dealing with vertical issues

table continues next page

Table 3.1 Romania Competition Council (RCC) Strategy and Key Metrics *(continued)*

Improve business process performance	**Optimize mandate on unfair competition** 1. New procedural rules introducing interim measure decisions and strict timeframe (max 3 months) to close the investigation 2. Establish Protocol of cooperation with National Audio-Visual Council 3. Legal framework modified to include "unfair commercial practices" within RCC mandate and remove overlaps with other agencies and institutions 4. Introduce sanction proportionate to the business function, i.e., behavioral and pecuniary	1. Number of cases reported to authorities 2. Number of "reasoned" complaints received by RCC 3. Number of decisions within 3 months as percentage of total cases initiated 4. Number of decisions which impose fines as percentage of total
Promote Romanian position in international cooperation	**Enhance state aid processes** 1. Strengthen ex post monitoring and impact of state aid schemes, including any distortive effects on competition 2. Mandatory consultation of the SA instrument and more weight given to RCC POV opinions 3. Increase visibility of RCC activity and closer contact with beneficiaries 4. Introduce obligation for the grantor to provide a cost-benefit analysis of the impact of the proposed measure in the market place	1. Number of state aid schemes with analysis of impact completed 2. Number of consultations in the design of State Aid instrument related to 3. Percentage of non-confidential notices published related to State aid review process
Guarantee effective enforcement	**Advance RCC business enablers** 1. Provide effective human resource management 2. Provide effective infrastructure and security management 3. In crease IT capabilities 4. Ensure effective financial and acquisition management	1. Percentage of staff turnover 2. Time for saving of routine HR and administrative paper work 3. Average number of training hours per employee 4. Number of electronic documents registered in a month 5. Number of case workflow events implemented using automated and auditable processes 6. Number of issues, incidents, complaints reported by users 7. System availability across the enterprise 8. Number of prevented information security breaches 9. Percentage of RCC staff who log into the CMS every day

Solutions

The World Bank recommended that roles of the RCC's Board and President be clearly defined and a new executive secretary be established. The Board is the decision-making body of the RCC. It operates as a permanent collegial body—whereby each member equally participates in RCC decisions within the RCC's structure. Board members would not be involved in any operational tasks, except when commissions delegate powers according to a predefined criterion. For example, one criterion for forming a delegation is that it be knowledge based. In such a case, the Board may delegate a commission made up of Board members with specialized knowledge. There will be a clear demarcation line between adjudication and operational functions. From a business point of view, the President will not be involved in operational processes, which will be run by investigative units and supervised by an executive secretary, a position established to guarantee the separation of functions. A cabinet will support each Board member, and the new executive secretary will ensure symmetry between the information provided to the President and to Board members. The case handler will be appointed by the director of the investigative unit, not the President. Governance reforms will improve the transparency and accountability of RCC operations.

Information Technology Environment

Challenges

The RCC's IT landscape is nascent. There are no IT strategies, principles, processes, or architectures within the RCC to define how IT can support business operations. The RCC's current IT use is minimal. Several Excel- and Word-based solutions exist to support users and some RCC processes, such as reporting, case tracking, and financial applications. But more specialized programs are not generally in use. Enterprise solutions are minimal, and most data are stored on local drives rather than enterprise-wide servers. There is no specialized IT staff to support the RCC's technology requirements; the IT forensics team provides this support in addition to its investigative functions.

Solutions

The World Bank Group's review of the technology architecture provides a plan for the RCC to improve its IT capabilities and optimize the value of its IT investments. The architecture plan provides four points of advice for building an IT framework:

- An IT strategy needs to be developed and anchored in a comprehensive definition of the scope and business objectives of the RCC. It requires a comprehensive plan of action for all IT investments, including clearly defined tradeoffs and institutional arrangements to execute the strategy.

- A future IT governance framework needs to provide strategic guidance and ensure that IT investments and operations align with institutional priorities. As the RCC increasingly depends on IT to improve its efficiency and effectiveness, there will be a need for greater accountability for technology-related decisions. So, IT governance must be a part of the RCC's overall governance framework.
- IT processes and procedures must be standardized. Operational standards for project management, quality assurance, enterprise architecture and information and technology management will ensure that performance matches service (box 3.1).
- A corporate function should manage and administer the RCC's IT, but skills for project management, architecture management, and solutions integration need to be developed.

Technology reforms will focus on how to use IT to improve RCC functions. Case management, financial management, and human resource management will be supported by common software technologies related to the management of documents, web content, infrastructure, management, and security and access management. Together, these technology solutions will help implement the RCC's goals, roles, and processes through standard frameworks, platforms, and software components.

Box 3.1 Basic IT Principles

Underlying the RCC's technology architecture and IT operations, 12 IT principles guide the use of all IT resources. The purpose is to ensure that the RCC's information environment is as productive, reliable, and cost-effective as possible.

1. IT investments are aligned with the RCC's strategic business priorities.
2. The IT department is responsible for implementing IT processes and infrastructure to meet user-defined requirements for cost, delivery, service levels, and functionality.
3. Information management processes must comply with all the relevant local, national, and international laws and policies.
4. Intellectual property must be protected.
5. Information is the most valuable asset.
6. Information must be secure.
7. The architecture defines the foundation for the future.
8. The architecture minimizes custom development (buy or build).
9. The architecture is based on common standards.
10. The architecture is service oriented.
11. Software and hardware should conform to defined standards that promote interoperability for data, applications, and technology.
12. Institutional systems are designed to be operational in the event of disruptions.

Revamping the operational framework requires developing a solution architecture and formulating "a migration plan" based on the business and technology architectures. The foregoing recommendations cannot be implemented all at once. Sharing information could be immediate, while building a strong IT environment will take years.[3] The solution architecture synthesizes the various recommendations into four core reforms related to strategy, governance, mandated functions, and IT (table 3.2). A phased approach to reforms, recommended and synthesized in the migration plan, will give the RCC the ability to identify clear targets and measure business values for each solution. The sequence of delivery is based on priorities, budgets, functional and technical dependencies, and organizational capabilities. Each step of the migration plan provides a completely functional structure to achieve the business objectives. It also builds on the business and technical components of previous phases and provides a foundation of business and technical objectives for future phases. The cost of carrying out the migration plan is about US$8 million over five years.

Results

The RCC has started to implement changes to its organizational structure.[4] RCC management has endorsed the World Bank recommendations and subsequently secured EU Funds[5] to implement the proposed reforms. By following the implementation roadmap,[6] the RCC is now well under way to improve its business architecture. A first step (Release 1) of the implementation roadmap entails the business reengineering and automation of the mergers processes, improving the capabilities of IT forensics, upgrading the IT infrastructure, and developing foundational software solutions to support the execution and monitoring of RCC operations. This was scheduled to be launched by the end of March 2015 (table 3.2).

The RCC also adopted several good practices. Dedicated staff from three different units in the Mergers department were assigned for the duration of the

Table 3.2 Reengineering and Automating the Merger Processes (Release 1)

Focus area	Changes adopted
Strategy	• Management information on merger activities is available through reports and a management dashboard. Monitoring and performance evaluation of merger activities and its alignment with the overall strategic framework can be tracked in real time.
Governance	• Resource accountabilities and responsibilities are now clearly defined and managed systematically. For example, RCC staff who should only be informed of activities are permitted only to view screens but cannot edit the data. 　○ The Head of Unit Merger is accountable for the overall merger review process, assigning the project team and signing-off on the findings and recommendations of the investigative team. 　○ The President and management will have access to the electronic dashboard that provides information on merger-review activities. They will be informed but not involved in the operational activities of reviewing mergers.

table continues next page

Table 3.2 **Reengineering and Automating the Merger Processes (Release 1)** *(continued)*

Focus area	Changes adopted

Mandated functions	• A standard registration process, created as a separate service, will be reused for all other RCC processes. Documents submitted and generated by the RCC are tagged and available to RCC staff on the basis of access rights.
	  ○ Documents submitted to the RCC are electronically scanned and archived. This allows for automatic retrieval, quick identification, and easy sharing of information and granting of permission rights.
	  ○ Confidential documents are tagged and managed electronically with the proper access controls.
	• Merger processes are streamlined.
	  ○ Simplified procedures are based on specific thresholds.
	  ○ Preliminary and official notification steps are standardized.
	  ○ Deadlines are systematized in accordance with EU practices.
	  ○ Workloads are distributed in accordance with predetermined criteria.
	  ○ Accountability is delegated to the lowest level in the process.
	  ○ Standardized checklists and forms are implemented to promote consistency across the RCC.
	• IT forensics was strengthened with new technologies and training in the use of these technologies.

Information technology	• Workstation upgrades for one-third of RCC staff, including those in the RCC's territorial offices. These workstations are standardized and should be easier to maintain. • An RCC data center now exists in the government data center and is managed to be highly available, with failover capabilities. • Standard software solutions were purchased for competition enforcement. They include document management, business process/business rule management, business intelligence, and IT infrastructure. They can be leveraged for subsequent implementation. • Web services that enable the exchange of information with relevant institutions/systems (for example, MoJ for Trade Registry, and SEAP for procurement data) were developed and can be leveraged for subsequent releases. • IT staffing has been strengthened with the recruitment of a senior IT professional and the creation of an open position (recruitment pending). • An IT governance framework was operationalized with the establishment of a steering committee, which comprises mid-level management. The committee provides timely decision making and issue resolution to facilitate business process reengineering and automating merger review and investigations.

project to work with external contractors, facilitating the standardization of merger processes. They worked closely with their colleagues and respective management to facilitate timely decision making and issue resolution. A project-steering committee comprising RCC mid-level management is guiding the project and addressing cross-cutting issues. The President and Board members of the RCC have visibly supported the reform process.

Several improvements in human resource development were reported in 2014. The induction of newly recruited officers led to faster integration into the RCC activity and internships were used to screen talent. Staff promotion was made more dynamic through a performance criterion (with an increased number of promotions in 2013 over the previous years). Desired competencies were introduced for teamwork; conflict management; decision making and problem solving; planning, organizing, and managing projects (for external relations and support departments); the legal competition framework (for the legal directorate); and planning and organizing (for management staff).

Moving Forward

Before initiating a project, RCC staff should "see" what the system can do for them and get a sense of how their work will "look" and how it would affect their day-to-day activities.[7] The implementation of "Release 1"[8] will provide the RCC with greater transparency in its activities (albeit limited to mergers in this phase). Simplified business processes and clearly defined accountabilities will improve efficiency at all levels. Well-defined timelines and alert mechanisms embedded in the system will improve the ability to monitor activities and workloads. The system will be implemented only for new merger reviews, so there will be a transition period as RCC staff continue with manual processes (to close existing reviews) but begin working with electronic systems where available. To facilitate the transition to the automated processes, the RCC's regulation for organization and functioning will be updated to reflect the changes. Management engagement in support of the RCC's modernization will continue; management reports from the system will form the basis for operational decisions and performance evaluation.

The automation of the sector inquiries, unfair competition, antitrust activities, and regulatory impact assessments should be prioritized and sequenced in the implementation plan. More advanced capabilities in using "big data" technologies—like analyzing procurement patterns to identify bid rigging—will enable the RCC to do more to foster competition. At a later stage, modernizing human resource and financial management must also be addressed.

Notes

1. Deliverables 3.1. Detailed Business Architecture—Current and Target, December 2014; 3.2. Target State

   Technology Architecture, January 2013; and 3.3. Target State Solution Architecture and Sequencing, July 2013.

2. For example, the flow of a case, from the triggering event until the Board decision, will be streamlined by distinguishing between preliminary reviews and official reviews. Each phase of the process will be implemented in accordance with automated procedural steps. Roles within the RCC will be predefined according to the RACI (Responsible, Accountable, Consulted, Informed) framework, and management tools will be used to delineate accountabilities. The RACI will be formalized in the RCC Regulation of Organization and Functioning and Operational Procedures and will define the roles and functions based on each mandated area of intervention (including antitrust, merger, and market inquiry). These rules will be reflected in the document classification and access rights to all the RCC's files (including documents and other evidence attached to files). Each RCC output will be configured in accordance with standardized forms to perform tasks in a "uniform house style." All official activities will be coded in an electronic case-management repository, enabling those with access rights to verify each institutional activity and generate reports. These reforms will make RCC processes more efficient

and reliable and increase the RCC's visibility and credibility with institutional stakeholders and market players.

3. To identify the scope and sequence of the reforms, the RCC decided to be guided based on several questions: (i) What is the business priority? (ii) what is the available budget? (iii) what is the level of functional or process reuse? (iv) what is the level of technology reuse? (v) what is the readiness of IT skills? (vi) what is the readiness of end-user skills? (vii) what legal or regulatory reforms are required?

4. RAS advice on the RCC organizational structure ("Enterprise Architecture") was completed by summer 2013.

5. The funding for the Interoperability project also supported the implementation of Release 1. Web services calls were developed to link the RCC with other institutions/systems that provide relevant information in the merger review, including the procurement system (SEAP) and trade registry (MoJ).

6. Presented in the "Solution Architecture" and the technical details elaborated in the "Technology Architecture."

7. For example, what happens when the document is scanned? Where does it go? How will I get to it? Providing insights into how the system may work will early in the process expose staff to the possibilities that they may not have envisioned.

8. RCC is requesting that the subsequent steps in the implementation roadmap be taken into consideration for the request of EU funds in the 2014–20 programming period. The implementation roadmap should therefore be reviewed and updated to reflect the priorities of the RCC. The lessons learned from the first implementation should be factored into the project implementation. Release 2.0 covers the automation of the remaining antitrust activities, market inquiry, and regulatory impact assessment. Release 3.0 automates the activities supporting Unfair Competition reviews, integration of Financial Management and HR Management and development of RCC's business intelligence platform (that is, Big Data). Release 4.0 will implement the remaining functional areas that have to be addressed including State Aid–Ex Ante, full integration of the HR and the Financial Management systems with RCC's core systems and expansion of the business intelligence platform (for example, early warning systems).

Building Landmarks, Smoothing Out Markets • http://dx.doi.org/10.1596/978-1-4648-0620-9

CHAPTER 4

Enforcing Competition Law

Preventing Anticompetitive Mergers

Challenges

Merger controls in Romania place unnecessary administrative burdens on businesses and preclude reallocating Romania Competition Council (RCC) resources to complex competition cases. Merger control policy should be designed and implemented to ensure that merger reviews are timely, efficient, and effective. This means that merger policy should prevent operations that reduce competition and minimize the burden of administrative procedures on businesses. The entry, growth, and exit of businesses in a given market are natural in a competitive business environment, so merger regulations should not obstruct these processes. [1]

Markets are not defined consistently properly, limiting the RCC's ability to analyze the impacts of mergers. A market definition that is too narrow could conclude that firms enjoy monopoly power or that certain mergers restrict competition. And a market definition that is too broad could conclude that abusive conduct by powerful firms does not have appreciable effects on the market. The paucity of relevant data often prevents the use of more sophisticated methodologies for defining antitrust markets. In Romania, a review of several merger decisions by the RCC indicates that market definitions were not proper. These mergers took place in 2012 in several markets, including lubricants, real estate, fuel distribution, medical care equipment, and equipment for gasoline stations. There was no discussion in the reviewed documents of a systematic analysis of what the relevant product was and whether it had any close substitutes. It was also unclear what evidence was used to determine geographic markets.

Solutions

The two goals of the analysis of merger reviews were to reduce the unnecessary administrative burdens on businesses and to reallocate resources freed by that process to more pressing competition issues and more complex cases. Streamlining merger procedures would allow the RCC to be more efficient while enhancing legal certainty for merging firms. This change in focus would be complemented by analytical tools that define relevant markets and estimate the effects of economic concentration.

Core recommendations involve regulatory amendments to merger laws and improving the RCC's implementation practices. Potential regulatory amendments include increasing merger thresholds to more adequately reflect the size of Romanian markets and enhancing the scope and functioning of the fast-track procedure. Even with low notification thresholds, only 33 percent of concentrations in Romania were reviewed under the simplified procedure, about half the 60 percent in the European Union (EU). Other recommendations include adopting official filing forms, making prenotification meetings more important, and consolidating RCC information requests issued during the merger review. These improvements need to be accompanied by a strengthened RCC analytical capacity—especially in defining relevant markets and estimating the effects of concentration.

Guidelines for economic analysis of mergers were developed to assist the RCC in reviewing the effects of mergers. They cover market definition, market structure and concentration, unilateral and coordinated effects of mergers, market entry and expansion, merger efficiencies, failing firms, and nonhorizontal mergers. The guidelines then apply these concepts to actual merger-review cases from the EU, Canada, and the United States.

A quick guide on the use of quantitative tools was developed to help define relevant markets. The guide discusses the applicability and limitations of market definitions and quantitative techniques. It also discusses two sets of quantitative techniques that are applied to price analyses and demand substitutability analyses. And it discusses practical examples where these techniques were used to define relevant product and geographic markets.

Results

A new merger regulation was adopted on September 30, 2014, introducing several changes. Greater importance will be placed on prior contacts between the RCC and the projects to submit merger notifications in a simplified form. Publishing information on merger notifications will allow stakeholders to express their views and increase the openness and transparency of RCC activities. And the use of simplified procedures will be expanded to concentrations unlikely to affect the competitive environment.

The Guide for Economic Analysis of Mergers has proven useful for the RCC's Economic Analysis Group. It provides a reference for carrying out economic analyses in merger cases, particularly in the analysis of the unilateral effects of mergers using indexes of upward price pressure and gross upward price pressure.

Fighting Exclusionary Business Practices

Challenges

The RCC's assessment of exclusionary practices[2] seldom analyzes the effects on consumers, increasing the risk that consumers will be hurt by exclusionary conduct.[3] Exclusionary business practices aim at (or have the effect of) weakening competition by excluding firms from entering the market or limiting the expansion of existing competitors. Such practices might be used by dominant firms to maintain or gain market power, with the ultimate goal of increasing prices and restricting supply. In the short run, consumer harm is manifested through higher prices and limited supply and choice. In the long run, the lack of competition implies less innovation, which could limit the introduction of new and improved products.

Exclusionary business practices that do not affect consumer welfare should not be deemed illegal. For example, the exclusion from the market of inefficient firms would not be illegal since it is not harmful for consumers and would happen even without any exclusionary conduct.

Solutions

The World Bank helped develop a guide to assist the RCC in analyzing the effects on consumers of the abuse of a dominant position. Drawing on the EU framework and international best practices, the guide presents a methodology to analyze the effects on competition and consumer welfare from predation, loyalty rebates, exclusive dealings, refusals to supply, margin squeezes, and bundling/tying. The expected outcome is for the RCC to replace existing legality tests, which assume that any restriction to competition by dominant firms will harm consumers, with sounder economic analysis that prioritizes cases that affect consumer welfare.

Ensuring Access to File and Confidentiality

While investigating antitrust cases, firms need to access relevant files and information on equal terms with authorities. A system of access to file should be designed so that it is timely, efficient and effective and adequately protects the confidentiality of information.[4]

Challenges

In Romania, overinclusive confidentiality policies, unsystematic organization of files, and the absence of strict deadlines during the investigation threaten the rights of defense of the parties. And the ability to appeal the decisions of the RCC, used by parties, delay proceedings, allows for the disclosure of confidential information in front of the court.

Solutions

The World Bank Group proposed a number of practical recommendations to enhance access to files and confidentiality policies. These include decriminalizing of leaking confidential information by RCC staff and developing internal guidance to make access to files and the treatment of confidentiality simpler and more efficient.

Fostering Deterrence: Fines, Leniency, and Cease and Desist

Important in an effective competition framework is the ability to deter anticompetitive practices. A strong combination of enforcement tools can foster deterrence and dissuade firms from enacting antitrust violations in the first place. High fines do more than punish the violator; they also dissuade other companies from violating the competition law. A well-functioning leniency program is not only crucial to destabilizing cartels by creating a permanent offer that any of its members may come forward to the authority to avoid fines. Such a program also deters cartel formation. Finally, cease-and-desist commitments can be used to settle cases quickly and efficiently, thus deterring firms from continuing with anticompetitive conducts.[5]

Challenges—Fines

Defining a clear and consistent fining methodology enhances transparency, impartiality and legal certainty for the private sector. In addition to being predictable, fines should be proportional in order to reflect the degree of gravity and the duration of the infringement. If expected fines for infringement are too low to deter, then enforcement activity is unproductive, while if they are too high, they will be seen as unjust and partial.

Solutions—Fines

The World Bank Group emphasized the need to link the RCC's fining policies with the broader goals of the agency, including implementing an effective leniency policy. Proposed regulatory amendments included calculating fines in relation to affected markets rather than the total world turnover of the undertaking, as well as eliminating minimum fines, now set at 0.5 percent of the total turnover (box 4.1).

Challenges—Leniency

Leniency programs can break the code of silence among cartel members and uncover conspiracies that might otherwise go undetected. Three preconditions

---

Box 4.1 Proposed Step-by-step Methodology to Calculate Fines

Step 1: Determine the base level according to the gravity and duration of the infringement.

$$x \text{ gravity} + y \text{ duration} = \text{base level}$$

Step 2: Adjust for aggravating or mitigating factors.

Step 3: Adjust for specific deterrence and proportionality.

Step 4: Adjust if the maximum penalty of 10 percent of the total turnover of the undertaking is exceeded.

Step 5: Apply reductions under the leniency program.

---

are necessary for an effective leniency program in Romania: high risk of detection, significant sanctions, and, for the effective operation of the program, transparency and certainty of prospective applicants.[6] For leniency to become successful in Romania, it is important to improve the balance between the cost and benefit of reporting on a cartel and the risks associated with both. At the moment, the RCC's leniency program is to some extent hindered by lengthy procedures as well as wasteful use of scarce resources, since leniency is not limited to hard-core cartels.

Solutions—Leniency

To address the shortcomings in leniency, the World Bank recommended focusing on hard-core cartels only while mainstreaming the procedural steps of the program in order to enhance the relevant legal information for potential applicants. Leniency rules should establish the right incentives to come forward as the first applicant, but benefits may arise from granting benefits to subsequent firms offering to cooperate with the RCC. This can be achieved not only through the leniency program itself but also through a strategic use of plea agreements.

Results—Leniency

New leniency guidelines have been approved by the RCC Board and cleared by the Legislative Council. But their adoption has been postponed due to legal issues regarding pending cartel cases that need to be addressed first.

Challenges—Cease and Desist

The lack of a comprehensive settlement policy hinders cartel deterrence and leads to an inefficient allocation of the RCC's resources. Settlements or plea agreements enable the RCC to swiftly and effectively close a case since they reward cooperation from the interested parties and can be used to create and sustain momentum in the investigation of other antitrust violators. Settlements can also be instrumental to complement a well-functioning leniency policy. They provide an important vehicle for resolving charges against those who have lost the leniency race.

Solutions—Cease and Desist

The recommendations of the World Bank Group aimed to enhance the use of this enforcement tool with a complementary legal regime to guide the RCC in determining the amount of a fine accessed on the violators in cases where they acknowledge the practice they have committed and are willing to accept a fine (with some bargaining possible on its amount). But this enforcement tool is absent from Romanian legislation, which only allows for a 10 percent to 30 percent reduction of a fine if the firms involved admit to their violation of the competition rules.

Results—Cease and Desist

Regarding procedural aspects related to the guidelines on the application of cease- and-desist commitments, the RCC modified the relevant sections. It expressly mentions the applicant's right to be informed of the results of the market test, the applicant's right to comment when the investigation was triggered by a complaint, and an extension of the deadline by which third parties may submit comments.

Minimizing Competition Distortions Associated with Granting State Aid

Challenges

The RCC needs to strengthen its analytical ability to carry out ex ante and ex post economic assessments of state aid. state aid decisions have traditionally been based on an ex ante analysis, with the general assumption that aid would bring about the intended effects. In the EU, the State Aid Modernization (SAM) initiative seeks to add to this approach and introduce an ex-post evaluation of state aid in the case of block-exempted aid schemes. This evaluation assesses the actual effects of the aid on markets, positive or negative. In this respect, ex post evaluations measure aid effectiveness, allowing for the evaluation of public spending and thus improving the efficiency of public interventions. While the ex-ante assessment balances the potential positive and negative effects of state aid and is necessary to ascertain its compatibility with the common market (Articles 107(2) and (3) and 108(3) Treaty on the Functioning of the European Union [TFEU]), the ex post evaluation is required for certain aid schemes that are large, novel, or face the possibility of significant (market, technological, or regulatory) change in the near future. Its function is therefore merely to measure the positive and negative effects on the market of state aid granted in the past and thus to design better (more efficient and less distortive) state aid in the future. A functional ex post evaluation involves the following steps: (i) verify the ex-ante assumptions that led to state aid approval; (ii) using performance indicators, assess the effectiveness of delivering stated objectives; (iii) assess unforeseen negative impacts and propose remedies; (iv) improve the design of schemes by taking these negative impacts into account. Ex post evaluation should contribute to better policy making, simplification of the process and an improved resource allocation.[7]

Solutions

The World Bank supported the development of a guide to provide the RCC with the analytical tools required to evaluate the impact of state aid. The guide would help ensure the transparency, effectiveness, and coherence of Romania's state aid measures (figure 4.1).

Figure 4.1 Dynamic Process of State Aid Assessment and Evaluation

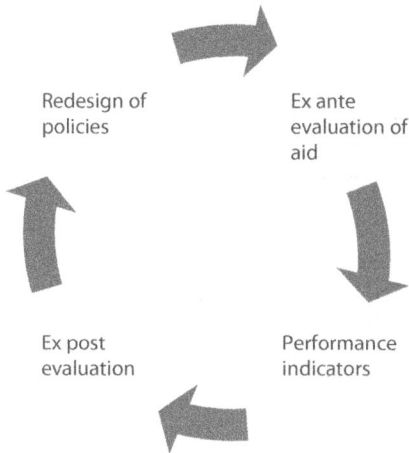

Redesign of
policies

Ex ante
evaluation of
aid

Ex post
evaluation

Performance
indicators

Capacity Building for Staff and Board Members

Challenges

Human resources are essential for knowledge-based organizations like the RCC. One of the key areas for improvement identified in the World Bank's 2010 Functional Review was the lack of clear investigative leadership and staffing that fully meets organizational needs. In 2013, the RCC employed 306 people, up 7 percent from 2011. Eighty percent of the budget is dedicated to salaries, demonstrating the importance assigned to human resources as a core asset. But transforming the RCC into a high-performing agency does not require expansion as much as enhancement of its agility and capabilities which, expressed more concisely, means building human capacity.

Solutions

The World Bank supports the development of RCC staff skills and the introduction of effective human resource management. It assessed the RCC's current human capacity and developed a training plan based on identified needs. The assessment acknowledges the need to strengthen both hard skills and soft skills. Hard skills include technical abilities—like carrying out economic analyses. Soft skills include more general abilities—like thriving on a team. It also tackled issues related to strengthening the recruitment and selection processes, specifically through (i) greater involvement of the HR Manager and the National Agency of Public Function (ANFP) representatives, (ii) trainings in recruitment techniques; (iii) using key performance indicators for the recruitment process; (iv) designing and implementing a successful induction/onboarding process; (v) creating greater transparency in the process of grade promotion and building a set of performance indicators; (vi) improving processes for setting staff objectives and performance evaluation and aligning them with the RCC's mission; (vii) setting development needs in a clearer, more prioritized and transparent way; (viii) incorporating development activities into a clearly defined Development Strategy; and (ix) building a set of key business indicators for the development process.

The training assessment identified the hard, specialized skills needed within the RCC. The skills, typically built over the medium term, require specialized education and practical training.

- Knowledge of the legal frameworks that govern competition is essential at all levels of the RCC. This knowledge includes understanding internal RCC procedures and relevant European and Romanian legislation and jurisprudence, which it applies to competition cases and investigations. About 100 staff members require these skills, and another 44 would benefit from having them.
- The ability to undertake economic research and analyses is important because most RCC decisions affect market conditions and ultimately consumer welfare. Economic analyses complement legal analyses and can reveal the effects of different business conducts on economic efficiency and consumer welfare. Several RCC functions require market definition and assessment of market power mergers, horizontal agreements, and vertical restraints.
- Investigative competency, fundamental for antitrust and merger activities, includes training in investigative methods, the ability to conduct professional interviews and the competence to carry out "dawn raids" to collect information at the offices of firms under investigation.
- RCC staff needs to use and understand information technology (IT) and digital evidence. IT forensics is the use of specialized techniques for the analysis, extraction, examination, preservation, authentication, interpretation, documentation, and identification of digital information. Staff need to examine residual data, reconstruct computer system usage, explain the technical features of data, authenticate data through technical analyses, and perform analyses on live computer systems.
- RCC staff should have sector- or industry-specific knowledge. This includes the ability to understand business models, market segmentation, main competitors, the jurisprudence of specific industries, responsibilities of other regulatory agencies, information from various sources, and the definitions and evolution of relevant markets and industries.

Demand is high for soft skills as well. These skills assure the efficient use of resources and maximize the impact of hard skills.

- A wide variety of communication skills include presentation, written communication, public speaking, and general communication like active listening, message structuring, and audience interaction.

- Teamwork needs to be encouraged, strengthened, and rewarded in the RCC to maximize the benefits of sharing information, experience, and best practices.
- Leadership skills are critical, especially for middle managers and case handlers, who need to lead both the tasks and their teams. They are required to foster strong relationships with internal and external stakeholders and encourage collaboration, knowledge sharing, and participatory decision making. Managers need to be able to deliver high-quality results on time and within budget.
- Good organizational skills are important, particularly for competition inspectors who need to plan, delegate tasks, and manage allocated resources to achieve an investigation's milestones.
- Foreign language skills are very close to becoming required skills. The RCC requires easy access to other countries' knowledge, materials, information, and best practices. For this, employees must be able to communicate in different languages. The language most requested is English, with French and German close behind.
- Crisis-management skills are important. Dawn raids and even case investigations can lead to conflicts and crisis situations, and RCC staff have to manage different conflict events without jeopardizing the scope and objectives of the mission.
- Management competencies are deemed crucial skills. RCC managers typically rely on their experience and knowledge of technical skills to lead, but they lack in-depth managerial training. They often do not effectively manage or delegate responsibilities.

In light of these training needs, the RCC and the World Bank developed a comprehensive training plan. The plan proposed a detailed roadmap and defined the structure, objectives, delivery methods, and evaluation tools for each training category. The training plan recommends measures to integrate the training policy into HR management policy and HR information systems. The plan takes into account certain reform restrictions that fall under the national legal framework that governs public sector employees in Romania.

The training plan includes many training activities. Through November 2014, there were 12 training courses offered that were attended by more than 170 RCC employees, for a total of about 1300 training days. Eight of the 15 training needs outlined in the training assessment were covered by 12 courses. Two-thirds of the participants in the training program attended one or two training courses, while the last third attended three or more training courses. The 12 training courses included the following (see also box 4.2):

1. For a Successful Change management: Balancing performance and strategy: four-day training session; July 29–August 1, 2013
2. Conducting dawn raids in practice, investigative methods, and forensics analysis: four-day training session; October 18–21, 2013

3. Economic Research and Analysis of market definition, abuse of dominance, and vertical restraints: three-day training session; December 9–12, 2013
4. Economic Research and Analysis of horizontal agreements, oligopolies, merger control, and intellectual property rights: three-day training session; March 11–14, 2014
5. Conducting dawn raids in practice, investigative methods, and forensics analysis: four-day training session; May 12–15, 2014
6. Effective Written Communication on competition topics: three-day training session; May 26–28, 2014
7. Leadership and Problem solving for antitrust investigators: three-day training session; May 29–31, 2014
8. Leadership and Problem solving for antitrust investigators: three-day training session; August 4–6, 2014
9. Principles of Competition and unfair competition law: four-day training session; August 11–14, 2014
10. Principles of Effective People Management and Communication: three-day training session; September 9–11, 2014
11. Competition Project Management: three-day training session, October 8–10, 2014
12. Comparative Competition Jurisprudence in EU Law: three-day training session; October 15–17, 2014.

Box 4.2 Snapshot of Selected Capacity Building Workshops

Workshops on Conducting Dawn Raids in Practice: Investigative Methods and IT Forensics Analysis

Dawn raids are increasingly regarded as key instruments in competition authorities' fight against cartels. However, they raise three specific legal and practical issues: (i) preparatory aspects, (ii) the actual conduct of the dawn raid (gathering of physical and digital evidence and interviewing and interrogation techniques), and (iii) the analysis of digital evidence through new IT forensic technologies. Two workshops on conducting practice dawn raids took place in Bucharest: the first, from November 18 to 21, 2003, and the second, between May 12 and May 15, 2014. The response to the workshop was overwhelmingly positive. The event participants obtained hands-on training on how the Federal Bureau of Investigation (FBI) and U.S. Department of Justice team up in the preparation, conducting and forensic analysis of evidence gathered in dawn raids. In particular, the participants received practical advice and gained valuable skills in IT forensics, drafting affidavits, and the technicalities of international cooperation between competition agencies.

The Economics Behind Competition Law: Intensive Training Courses

Economics are fundamental for understanding the rationale behind competition law. It is therefore unsurprising that the interpretation and application of economic theories and

box continues next page

Box 4.2 Snapshot of Selected Capacity Building Workshops *(continued)*

concepts plays an increasingly central role in the decision-making process of competition agencies in Europe and across the world. In order to understand the way in which economic reasoning is used by parties and decision makers, the World Bank organized two trainings with speakers from Compass Lexecon, R&P Economics, and RBB Economics. The first training, which took place between December 9 and 12, 2013, focused on (i) market power and market definition; (ii) pricing and nonpricing abusive practices; (iii) the interaction between competition and regulation, and (iv) vertical restraint issues. This was followed by a second training with an emphasis on (i) horizontal agreements, (ii) oligopolistic behavior, (iii) merger control, and (iv) the intersections between IP rights and Competition law.

Workshop on Comparative Competition Jurisprudence in EU Law
EU Competition rules are directly applicable in Romania and both the RCC and the national courts are competent to apply them in cases that affect trade between Member States. The goal of this workshop was to strengthen the RCC's knowledge of EU Law in order to enable case handlers to align their case analysis with that of the Commission's institutions and to deliver decisions based on a sound legal analysis. The training, which took place between October 15 and 17, 2004, was presented by speakers from the Law firm Cleary Gottlieb, Steen & Hamilton. The training provided a comprehensive overview of the TFEU's rules on competition and the fundamental case law and Commission's practice in the fields of (i) horizontal agreements, (ii) abuse of dominance and (iii) merger control.

Principles of Unfair and Competition Law: Intensive Training Course
The RCC's model of the decentralized application of Competition law across Romania's territory requires a solid knowledge of the fundamentals of Competition law and Unfair Competition law by the RCC's regional offices. In order to help the RCC harmonize the application of Romanian and EU Competition law across its offices, a specific training on principles of Competition law was delivered by a speaker from the European University Institute on August 11 and 12, 2014. The training offered the participants a comprehensive analysis of Competition law principles in the areas of anticompetitive horizontal and vertical agreements, merger control, and the abuse of dominance. The participants' response to the trainings was overwhelmingly positive because of the constant interaction between speakers and participants. During the training, presentations were complemented with practical examples drawing on real cases brought before the European Commission and European courts. During these interactive exercises, participants were divided into groups and asked to play different roles, which would help them better understand and anticipate problems in their own work. Each day of training culminated with group exercises in which participants located what they learned and constructively presented ways to improve the RCC's enforcement capacities.

Results

A recent impact assessment of RCC training found that staff displays core strengths. The analytical skills that were acquired during capacity building workshops and advocacy events have already been used in recent antitrust cases. They have also been used in market inquiries to identify specific competition constraints, and to review projects with state aid elements. RCC staff possesses solid capacity to build collaborative relationships and can work as part of a team. They are ready to take charge of complex assignments. They are trustworthy and motivated to deliver high-quality services. Several soft skills—such as teamwork, leadership skills, dealing with organizational changes, and writing and presentation skills—have improved as a result of the capacity building. The assessment also suggests that staff members solve problems and make decisions on the basis of sound evidence, analysis, experience, creativity, and judgment. The RCC expects these personal strengths to support future learning activities.

Moving Forward

The impact assessment identified training opportunities to address persistent skill deficiencies. One type of training would aim to improve the RCC's capacity to conduct evidence-based analysis. A second would support efforts to better regulate certain sectors of the economy. A third would help managers lead and manage teams. A fourth would help RCC staff effectively communicate and represent the RCC before stakeholders and the public.

Activities are planned in 2015 to address development gaps and continue the reform momentum. The activities include arranging international study tours and internships to share experiences, planning advocacy initiatives with broad participation, and finalizing an IT architecture that modernizes the RCC's digital efforts. The RCC's mission, vision, and strategic goals will be consistent references to inspire staff motivation and enthusiasm. Competency-based staffing policies will be implemented, including competency-related key performance indicators as part of annual performance evaluations. A formal mentoring program and developmental assignments will encourage on-the-job training.

Notes

1. Deliverable 1.3.1.a: Law enforcement on mergers, merger regulations, and procedures, June 2013; Deliverable 1.3.1.b: Guidelines for economic analysis of mergers, July 2013; and Deliverable 1.3.5: Quick Guide on quantitative tools for defining relevant market, April 2014.

2. Exclusionary practices include predation, loyalty rebates, exclusive dealing, refusal to supply, margin squeeze, and bundling/tying

3. Deliverable 1.3.6: Guide on the analysis of effects of abuse of dominant positions on consumers, April 2014.

4. Deliverable 1.2.1: Technical report on the enhancement RCC regulations on access to file and confidentiality of information, January 2013, and Deliverable 1.2.2: Internal Guidance on procedures to determine confidentiality, January 2013.

5. 1.3.2.c and 1.3.2.d: Fining regulations and Guidelines, 1.3.2.a Comments to anticompetitive practices: leniency and 1.3.2.b Comments on Regulations and Guidelines for the application of cease and desist commitments

6. See chapter 2, p. 2, of the International competition network manual on cartel enforcement: "Drafting and implementing an effective leniency policy" (May 2009). Available at http://www.internationalcompetitionnetwork.org/uploads/library/doc341.pdf (last accessed May 3, 2013Id. at p. 2.

7. Deliverable 1.3.4: Methodological Guide for assessing the impact of granted state aid under current state aid legislation, September 2014.

CHAPTER 5

Creating a Competition Culture

Introduction

Competition advocacy promotes a competition culture through mechanisms beyond enforcement. The ability to raise awareness and issue opinions when policies, laws, or regulations can impair competition is at the core of ensuring competitive and open markets. According to the World Bank, competition advocacy has led to many quantifiable benefits. In the Arab Republic of Egypt, the price of steel rebar declined by half. In Mexico, the government saved approximately US$4.5 billion in public tenders. In Pakistan, an advocacy initiative saved pilgrims, partaking in the hajj, an estimated $60 million in airfares.[1] In Chile, 73 percent of the legal community responded in a survey that competition advocacy encouraged more competitive business behavior.[2]

Challenges

Awareness Raising for the Private and Public Sectors and Capacity Building for Stakeholders

In Romania public sector knowledge and commitment to competitive market principles were deemed not as extensive as they could be.

Competition advocacy complements the Romania Competition Council (RCC)'s enforcement capacity. The RCC has a powerful mandate to perform a wide array of competition advocacy activities, in line with competition agencies in the European Union (EU) and the United States, which can comment on legislative and regulatory proposals and advocate for new ones. The RCC can provide opinions on the potential anticompetitive effect of legislation and regulations on markets. Competition inquiries identify market distortions and anticompetitive regulations. Cooperation protocols between sector-specific regulatory agencies and competition authorities can be useful for sharing information and coordinating activities. Awareness-raising campaigns can involve the courts, academia, and other public sector and private sector stakeholders. The general goal is to change the mindsets of market players and infuse competition principles into key sectors of the economy.

Collaboration with Regulators

Enhanced coordination between competition agencies and sectoral regulators can reduce the cost of doing business and enhance legal certainty. Memoranda of understanding can help competition agencies harmonize enforcement actions against anticompetitive practices in regulated sectors, such as telecom, electricity, transport, and public procurement and infuse competition into the regulatory framework of these sectors. The RCC has agreements with sector regulators, but they remain inactive because they lack a well-defined framework for cooperation. To tackle the most harmful anticompetitive practices, collaboration between the RCC and the Prosecutor's Office is also very important. [3]

Solutions

With the World Bank, the RCC carried out a number of competition advocacy events. These entailed around 1200 human-days of skills acquired and covered detecting bid rigging in public procurement, detecting cartels, competition law compliance and leniency, unfair competition, information technology forensics, and competition law. These events have the added benefit of raising the visibility of the RCC, especially in situations relevant to strengthening links between competition policy and other policies, such as public procurement. Public and private stakeholders—such as judges, academics, public procurement officials, and private law firms specializing in competition law—have benefited from in-depth discussions on key competition policy topics (box 5.1).

Box 5.1 Snapshot of Competition Advocacy Events

Prevention and Detection of Bid Rigging in Public Procurement—December 4–5, 2012
Enhancing the public procurement framework helps public authorities delivering high-quality goods and services at the lowest possible price, therefore achieving the best financial value. This event offered an in-depth analysis of how to effectively implement bid-rigging detection techniques and design pro-competitive tendering processes that mitigate the risks of bid rigging. The event's sessions included presentations by an Organisation for Economic Co-operation and Development (OECD) expert in bid rigging and by a highly reputed economics professor from New York University (US), who shared state of the art insights and practical advice on the detection of bid rigging, namely through screening techniques, and in the design procurement procedures that minimize the risk of bid rigging.

Cartel Detection April 25–26, 2013
Well-functioning cartel enforcement systems pose a threat to cartel members and make anticompetitive agreements among cartels more difficult. This event provided an overview of best practices from two of the top enforcement agencies in the world: the Netherlands Competition Authority (Autoriteit Consument & Markt stelt consument) and the Antitrust

box continues next page

Box 5.1 Snapshot of Competition Advocacy Events *(continued)*

Division of the U.S. Department of Justice. The sessions were designed to tackle practical aspects of cartel enforcement. These aspects included how to perform dawn raids, how to collect and analyze evidence, how to interrogate suspects and witnesses, how to carry out effective investigations, and how to work with whistleblowers within the leniency program. The final session was devoted to the economics of cartels.

Compliance and Leniency—June 27, 2013

Strengthening competition culture requires the private sector to play an active role in the enforcement of antitrust rules. This event provided an overview of key aspects of complying with competition law and the leniency program. It also discussed European and international practices from three top enforcement agencies: the UK Office of Fair Trading; the Netherlands Competition Authority (Autoriteit Consument & Markt stelt consument) and the Israel Antitrust Authority. The sessions were designed to tackle practical aspects of compliance with the competition laws and leniency programs that have been enacted in different countries. The goal was to provide guidance to the private sector on how to adopt a proactive position toward competition law enforcement.

Unfair Competition—May 8–9, 2014

A full-fledged Unfair Competition legal framework helps preserve fair competition in the market while guaranteeing a high level of consumer protection against misleading and aggressive marketing practices. This event provided a platform to discuss the most recent legislative proposals to amend the Romanian Unfair Competition Law with the RCC staff, academia and private-sector stakeholders. The sessions built upon the commentary to the Law proposal drafted by the renowned experts in unfair competition, Dr. Stefan Koos and Dr. Michael Bohner.

IT Forensics—May 15–16, 2014

In this digital age, IT Forensics is increasingly regarded as a key instrument in Competition Agencies' fight against cartels worldwide. This event provided hands-on training by the Antitrust Division of the U.S. Department of Justice. The sessions provided the participants with an applied methodology for gathering digital data, finding the probative bits and then presenting the results in a human readable format. The objective of the training was to share the Department of Justice's skills in the context of RCC's Laboratory using the FTK software.

EU Competition Law—October 24–25, 2014

EU Competition rules are directly applicable in Romania and both the RCC and the national courts are competent to apply them in cases that affect trade between Member States. This event provided an in-depth analysis of the application of Articles 101 and 102 Treaty on the Functioning of the European Union (TFEU) at the national level and counted with the presence of Judges from the European Courts and renowned European and Romanian academic experts. The goal of the Competition law conference was to strengthen the capacities of the RCC in applying the competition rules set forth in the TFEU and to fine-tune its economic approach to Competition law in line with EU law.

Further, the work of the World Bank Group focused on detecting gaps in the existing protocols and proposing a uniform framework of collaboration. First, an analytical note was produced to review the existing protocols signed by the RCC.[4] This note identifies the sectors where cooperation was most needed, including energy, communications, public procurement, and consumer protection, and then discusses possible tools to implement such cooperation more effectively. The options ranged from joint market enquiries to the creation of joint working groups on specific topics like merger approval or regulatory analysis. Finally, the note strengthens the importance of common training and capacity-building activities to develop mutual expertise. Second, the World Bank Group drafted a total of eight protocols implementing the above recommendations. Key aspects covered by the draft protocols include (1) enhanced consultation mechanisms in the context of merger analysis, state aid, and unfair commercial practices; (2) consistent procedural rules on confidentiality, information sharing, allocation, and transferring cases to the competent authority; and (3) definition of clear mechanisms to communicate through periodical meetings and technical focal points.

Results

In order to pursue systematic screening of potential bid rigging and cartel behavior and to promote competition in Romanian markets, the RCC is applying cartel-screening techniques acquired during the advocacy event on bid rigging. It is producing an internal guide for market screening and conducts a market analysis of beer producers in Romania based on the techniques learned.

Notes

1. https://www.wbginvestmentclimate.org/publications/the-competition-policy-advocacy-awards.cfm

2. https://www.wbginvestmentclimate.org/publications/the-competition-policy-advocacy-awards.cfm

3. Deliverable 1.4: Revision of protocols signed by the Romanian Competition Council, July 2013; Deliverable 1.4.1: Draft Protocol between the RCC and ANRE (Energy Regulatory Agency) and Recommendations for an Action Plan, July 2013; Deliverable 1.4.2: Protocol between the RCC and ANCOM, July 2013; Deliverable 1.4.3: Draft Model protocol with the National Agency for Medicines (ANM), July 2013; Deliverable 1.4.5: Draft Model protocol with the National Securities Commission, July 2013; Deliverable 1.4.6: Draft Model protocol with the National Regulatory Authority for Municipal Services (ANRSC), July 2013; Deliverable 1.4.7: Draft Model protocol with the National Regulatory Authority for Public Procurement (ANRMAP), July 2013; Deliverable 1.4.8: Draft Model protocol with the National Consumer Protection Authority (ANPC), July 2013 and Deliverable 1.5: Draft Model protocol for cooperation with the Prosecutor's Office attached to the High Court of Cassation and Justice (POHCJJ).

4. The World Bank revised 10 protocols with ANCOM (the National Authority for Communications) (2010), ANCP (the Consumer Protection Agency) (2006, 2007, 2009), ANM (the National Drug Agency) (2009), ANRE (the Energy Regulatory Agency) (2004), ANRMAP (the Public Procurement Authority) (2010), ANRSC(the Community Services of Public Utility Authority) (2005), CNVM (the Securities Authority) (2004), CSA (the Insurance Authority) (2004) and former CNVM and CSA, which were merged into the Authority for Financial Supervision (ASF).

RAS Experts

Table A.1 RAS Experts

Name	Surname	Position	Institution
Arabela Sena	Aprahamian	Senior Operations Officer, Task Team Leader	World Bank Group, Trade and Competitiveness Global Practice (GTCDR)
Gonçalo Miguel	Banha Coelho	Consultant	World Bank—GTCDR
Tania Priscilla	Begazo Gomez	Economist	World Bank—GTCDR
Michael	Bohne	Professor/Lawyer	University of Applied Sciences Offenburg
Andre	Brantz	Lawyer/Ex-Legal Counsel	Competition Law Division, Canadian Department of Justice
Jose Luis	Buendia Sierra	Lawyer Partner	Garrigues Law Firm, Brussels
Antonio	Capobianco	Senior Expert in Competition Law	OECD
Cesar	Chaparro Yedro	Private Sector Development Specialist.	World Bank—DECSI
Laurent Marie	De Muyter	Lawyer	Jones Day Law Firm, Brussels
Donato	De Rosa	Senior Economist	World Bank —GMFDR
Juan	Delgado Urdanibia	Founder and Director/ Senior Economist	R&P Economics, Madrid, Spain
Delia	Pierantonio	Associate	Cleary Gottlieb Law Firm, Rome,-Italy
Mihail	Dragoi	HR Expert	HR Dimensions Consulting Firm, Bucharest, Romania
Susan Pick	Dubas	Consultant	World Bank—ITSBI
Serge	Durande	Lawyer/Hearing Officer for Commissioners Monti and Kroes	Bird & Bird Law Firm Brussel/European Commission
Metz Rosa	Fontes De Abrantes	Professor/Economist	NYU—Stern Business School/Global Economics Group, New York, US
Ian Stewart	Forrester	Partner	White & Case Law Firm, Brussels
Andrea Filippo	Gagliardi	Senior International Competition Lawyer	EU/ACE Consultores,
Corina	Gazdoiu	Analyst	Consultant
Luisita	Guanlao	Lead Information Officer	World Bank—ITSQS

table continues next page

Table A.1 RAS Experts *(continued)*

Name	Surname	Position	Institution
Dany	Jones	IT Officer, Business Solutions II	World Bank—ITSQS
Diana	Kane	Trial Attorney	U.S. Department of Justice—Antitrust Department
Stefan	Koos	Law Professor	Academy of Administration and Economy, Munich, Germany
Robert Giles	Lancop	Economist	Competition Bureau of Canada
Francisco	Marcos Fernandez	Law Professor	Instituto de Empresa, IE Business School, Madrid, Spain
Federico Maria	Marini Balestra	Associate Resident	Cleary Gottlieb Law Firm, Rome, Italy
Mel Jacob	Marquis	Law Professor	Law Department, European University Institute, Florence, Italy
Martha	Martinez Licetti	Senior Economist	World Bank—GTCDR
Nancy Hall	Mcmillen	Trial Attorney	U.S. Department of Justice—Antitrust Department
Carmen Elena	Mincu	Professor/HR Expert	ASEBUSS—The Institute for Business Administration in Bucharest
Graciela	Miralles Murciego	Lawyer Comp 1 Coordination	World Bank—GTCDR
Claudia Silvia	Mirica	Internal Communication & Synergy Consultant	Consultant
Ronald	Myers	Public Administration Senior Expert	World Bank—GENDR
Peter Michael	Eugene	IT Expert	
Ana Florina	Pirlea	Analyst	World Bank—GTCDR
Georgiana	Pop	Economist Comp 1, 2 and 4 Coordination	World Bank—GTCDR
Denisa	Popescu	Senior IT Officer, Data and Information Management II	World Bank— ITSQS
Madalina	Pruna	Consultant	World Bank—GTCTI
Steven	Reichenbach	Senior Enterprise Architect	World Bank— ITSQS
Arthur Joseph	Riel	Director	World Bank—ITSME
Michel	Rogy	Senior ICT Policy Specialist	World Bank—GTIDR
Michael Joachim	Saller	Competition Expert	Bundenkartellamt, Bonn, Germany
Khaled	Sherif	Chief Admin. Officer	World Bank—BPSGR
Evgenia	Shumilkina	Results Measurement Specialist	World Bank—CGEDR
Silvia	Solidoro	Consultant	World Bank—GTCIS
Alexandru Cristian	Stanescu	Operations Analyst	World Bank—GTCDR
Mariana	Tavares De Araujo	Antitrust Lawyer/Partner	Levy Salomao Law Firm, Rio de Janeiro, Brazil

table continues next page

Table A.1 RAS Experts *(continued)*

Name	Surname	Position	Institution
Edwin Jozef	Van Dijk	Head of the Investigations Department	Authority for Consumers and Markets, Netherlands
Marcus Maria	Van Kordelaar	Lawyer	Authority for Consumers and Markets, Netherlands
Alexandre	Verheyden	Lawyer/Partner	Jones Day Law Firm,Brussels
Mark	Krotoski	Ex-Prosecutor	U.S. Department of Justice, Antitrust Department
John	Cauthen	Forensics Analyst/ Cyber Investigations	FBI/Government Accountability Office, U.S.
Ovie	Carroll	Director Cybercrime Lab	US Department of Justice, Computer Crime and Intellectual Property Section
Vitaly	Pruzanski	Principal Economist	RBB Economics, Brussels
Enrique	Canizares	Principal Economist	RBB Economics, Madrid, Spain
Lorenzo	Coppi	Senior Vice President	Compass Lexecon, London, UK
Stefano	Trento	Senior Economist	Compass Lexecon, London, UK
Elisabetta	Righini	Visiting Professor	Centre of European Law, The Dickson Poon School of Law, King's College, London
Gadi	Perl	Team Leader	Israeli Antitrust Investigations and Intelligence Department, Tel Aviv
Miara	Moran	Lawyer	Legal Department, Israel Antitrust Authority, Tel Aviv
Miriam	Van Heiningen	Lawyer	Authority for Consumers and Markets, Netherlands
Julien Henri	Stuyck	Law Professor	Leuven University, Netherlands
Catalin Stefan	Rusu	Law Professor	Radboud University, Nijmegen, Netherlands
Jean-Marc	Thouvenin	Law Professor	Paris Ouest Nanterre La Défense, France
Monika	Papp	Law Professor	Oetovos Lorand University, Hungary
Anna	Gerbrandy	Law Professor	Utrecht University, Netherlands
Peter Michael	Whelan	Law Professor	Leeds University, UK
Csongor	Nagy	Law Professor	Szeged University, Hungary
Anthony Michael	Collins	Judge	European Court of Justice, Luxembourg
Razvan	Antonescu	Communication Expert	World Bank

RAS Deliverables

Table B.1 RAS Deliverables

Component 1: Review of the legal and regulatory framework governing market competition

	Problem	Description of the problem	Deliverable to address the problem	Changes implemented
1.1.1 Report on Recommendations to amend the Unfair Competition law	Increased costs for businesses as a result of the lack of clarity and predictability in the enforcement of unfair Competition Law; RCC's resources are inefficiently used due to the lack of case prioritization.	Inconsistent approach to unfair competition with loopholes between different pieces of legislation and unclear definition of the competence of RCC vis-à-vis other agencies and both civil and criminal jurisdictions. Specific problems include (i) RCC's overlapping competences with other agencies in the field of Unfair Competition law; (ii) RCC's limited qualified resources to deal with unfair competition cases at the local level; (iii) no criterion to prioritize RCC's intervention; (iv) no clear distinction between unfair prices and predatory pricing; and (v) no harmonization of unfair competition sanctions with the criminal code.	Report on Recommendations to Amend the Unfair Competition law proposing (i) a general law on unfair competition applicable to all B2B activities; (ii) clear definition of RCC's competences based on an appreciability and an opportunity test and (iii) a consistent approach toward Unfair Competition Law in order to avoid loopholes between different pieces of legislation.	The Recommendations made were adopted through Government Ordinance 12/2014 on modifying Law 11/1990 on fighting unfair competition in August 2014. Ordinance 12/2014 incorporates core RAS recommendations, including an "opportunity test" to trigger RCC's competence (that is, public interest or the market structure must be affected) and a general unfair competition law catch-all clause. Furthermore, it offers a clearer definition of the purpose of the law and aligns the terminology used with EU law. In addition to Ordinance 12/2014, the RCC has enacted a Procedural Regulation in November 2014, which clarifies the opportunity test and issues of capacity to submit complaints with the RCC.
1.1.2 Analysis and Review of the State aid legal and regulatory framework	Risk of increased administrative discretion and of market distortions stemming from the lack of clarity of RCC role in the state aid area vis-à-vis granting authorities and courts	Romanian legislation is not fully in line with EU law and the Modernization of state aid rules and could be further clarified for the benefit of granting authorities, national courts, potential beneficiaries and competitors. In particular: (i) the procedure to grant aid and the obligations of the granting public authorities and the beneficiaries	Proposal of modifications to strengthen the Romanian State aid regulatory framework and bring it in line with EU law. The recommendations made in the Report include (i) clarification of the obligations of granting authorities; (ii) detailing the obligations imposed on beneficiaries of state aid; (iii) clarification of the procedural rules applicable to block-exempted state aid; (iv) further regulating the	WB recommendations were assessed and taken into account and discussed prior to the enactment of the Emergency Ordinance 77/2014 on state aid national procedures, which clarifies aspects related to state aid notification, obligations of state aid–granting authorities, aid recovery, the role of national courts, and de minimis aid.

table continues next page

Table B.1 RAS Deliverables (continued)

Component 1: Review of the legal and regulatory framework governing market competition	Problem	Description of the problem	Deliverable to address the problem	Changes implemented
		of state aid are not fully developed; (ii) no reference is made to the position of national courts in state aid cases; (iii) there are unclear obligations in terms of ex ante cost-benefit analysis and ex post monitoring; and (iv) scant reference is made to the procedural obligations imposed by the Block Exemption and de minimis Regulations.	recovery process with respect to unlawful aid; (v) stressing the role of national courts in state aid cases; (vi) improving awareness raising by the RCC on state aid matters; and (vii) devoting sufficient resources to the RCC on state aid matters.	
1.1.3: Recommendations to strengthen the Romanian Competition Law	Inability of the RCC to prioritize cases and undue burden on the private sector that increases the costs of doing business as a result of unclear provisions and unnecessary administrative steps in the RCL.	The RCL (i) does not allow the RCC to focus on public– interest cases and policies coherent with the agency priorities; (ii) foresees a significant amount of decisions that need to be taken internally by the President of the RCC and externally by the Bucharest Court of Appeals; (iii) establishes a 40% presumption	Proposal of several amendments to the Romanian Competition Law aimed at (i) empowering the RCC to focus on cases and mergers that are coherent with its priorities and that have a greater impact on Competition law and develop fast-track procedures for less important mergers; (ii) enhancing procedural effectiveness through the de-judicialization of competition enforcement; iii) reducing unnecessary burdens	The new Competition law draft which is still pending approval plans to (i) eliminate the threshold with a presumption of dominance; (ii) provide greater legal certainty to undertakings by clarifying the provisions regarding deadlines and prescription terms, by further aligning Articles 5 and 6 with Articles 101 and 102 TFEU; (iii) remove the possibility of price controls; (iv) limit the challenge before

table continues next page

Table B.1 RAS Deliverables *(continued)*

Component 1: Review of the legal and regulatory framework governing market competition

	Problem	Description of the problem	Deliverable to address the problem	Changes implemented
		of dominance; (iv) sets burdensome merger review procedures, including low notification thresholds, onerous information requests, and long review periods; has burdensome rules in terms of confidential information which favor the adoption of dilatory tactics; (v) has unclear advocacy powers; (vi) does not provide guidance in terms of RCC's interventions vis-à-vis price controls; and (vii) lacks criteria to determine sanctions for the infringement of competition.	(on the private sector, namely by clarifying the obligation to consult with the Supreme Council of National Defense, better articulating RCL with the TFEU and by deleting the 40% presumption of dominance; (iv) improving RCC's enforcement and sanctioning powers, namely by replacing "total turnover" by "affected turnover" and by encouraging the Prosecutor's office to criminally prosecute cartels; (v) removing government's ability to impose price controls; (vi) creating a "Hearing Officer" to deal with confidentiality issues; and (vii) clarifying and limiting the role of the President in privilege matters, while assigning some of its day-to-day operations to a neutral registry.	the Court of Appeal to RCC's final decisions on access to file and confidentiality; (v) create a position of Independent Procedural Officer specialized in the disposition of access to file, confidentiality, and other procedural matters separate to the enforcement team with the RCC; (vi) further clarify the provisions regarding legal privilege; and (vii) further clarify the rules on sanctions (please specify).
1.1.4. Review of the Legal and Regulatory Framework Governing Market Competition—Review of the Railways Legislation Package	Not fully efficient functioning of the railways market stemming from insufficient accounting separation between rail infrastructure and railways services.	The railways legislation lacked clarity and guidance on the following elements: (i) scope of the powers and competences of the RSC; (ii) RSC's access charges for rail tracks and related services; and (iii) compensation of public service contracts for passenger rail services.	Proposals with amendments to Romanian railways in line with EU law: (i) extending the powers and competences of the RSC; (ii) extending the services to be provided by the infrastructure manager; (iii) increasing transparency for entering the railway market; (iv) strengthening the "financial structure" of the railways sector; (v) requiring more accurate infrastructure charging rules; and (vi) providing guidance on the determination of compensation for public service contracts.	The RSC endorsed, together with the Ministry of Justice, a draft law initiated by the Ministry of Transport that will implement the EU Recast Directive.

table continues next page

Table B.1 RAS Deliverables *(continued)*

Component 1: Review of the legal and regulatory framework governing market competition

	Problem	Description of the problem	Deliverable to address the problem	Changes implemented
1.2.1 Technical Report on the enhancement of RCC's regulations on access to file and confidentiality of information	Undue burden on the private sector that boosts the costs of doing business as a result of an overly lengthy and unclear system of access to file/ confidentiality of information.	RCC's treatment of confidential information is not fully developed and lacks clarity in the following areas: (i) case handlers' concern of incurring criminal liability in case of release of confidential information; (ii) dilatory tactics by the parties when appealing the decisions of the RCC President granting access to confidential information; and (iii) no selection of relevant information when the file and other issues of internal organization are being assembled.	Report with theoretical and practical solutions to the problems faced by RCC when dealing with access to files and claims of confidential information in antitrust procedures. These actions include (i) establishing clear deadlines; (ii) dismissing irrelevant information gathered during an investigation; and (iii) following the principle of good administration when dealing with multiple-party cases and unfounded or exclusively dilatory requests.	
1.2.2. Internal Guidance and Procedures to determine confidentiality		Lack of consistency in the classification of confidential information by RCC makes proceedings unduly lengthy, unclear and prone to litigation in a way that reduces the effectiveness of Competition law enforcement.	Comments to the Romanian internal guidance and procedures to improve the effectiveness of treatment of confidentiality and access to files. The comments include (i) measures to facilitate the selection of relevant information and (ii) the purging of confidential information from a decision.	
1.3.1.a: Law enforcement on mergers: merger regulations and procedures	Unnecessary administrative burden on businesses associated with merger review while the RCC has to dedicate a large part of its resources to analyzing mergers with low potential to affect market competition and harm consumers.	The merger regulatory framework is not fully efficient due to (i) low merger notification thresholds contained in the RCL; (ii) lack of mechanism for review and adjustment of merger notification thresholds on a regular basis; (iii) inefficient internal procedures to review mergers; (iv) lack of official notification forms; (v) lack of guidance on pre-notification contacts; and (vi) absence of clear and transparent confidentiality policies.	Proposal with recommendations to amend Romania's merger regulations and procedures, including (i) removing merger thresholds from the RCL; (ii) setting merger-filing thresholds that ensure merging parties are of a significant size; (iii) reviewing merger thresholds on a regular basis; (iv) enhancing the scope and functioning of the fast-track procedure; (v) eliminating the assessment of whether a merger constitutes a threat to national security; vi) Consolidating RCC requests	A new merger regulation was adopted on September 30, 2014, introducing the following changes: (i) greater importance and scope of prior contacts between the RCC and the undertakings intending to submit notifications in a simplified form; (ii) increased openness and transparency of the RCC by publishing information on all merger notifications, in order to allow stakeholders to express their views; and (iii) extension of the scope of simplified procedures to concentrations that are not likely to affect the competitive environment.

table continues next page

Table B.1 **RAS Deliverables** *(continued)*

Component 1: Review of the legal and regulatory framework governing market competition	Problem	Description of the problem	Deliverable to address the problem	Changes implemented
			for information to parties during the merger review; (vii) formulating information requests proportionate to the complexity of the analysis in order to avoid generating undue costs for businesses; (viii) strengthening pre-notification consultations; (ix) adopting clearer filing form;s and (x) implementing more transparent confidentiality policies.	The new draft RCL is expected to remove the merger notification thresholds from its text and include them in a different type of legal act that can be regularly updated without cumbersome legislative procedures.
1.3.1.b Guide for economic analysis of mergers	Unclear market impact of anticompetitive mergers associated with higher prices/supply limitations, especially for consumers.	Evidence suggests that the RCC performs little economic analysis of mergers, particularly in terms of defining relevant markets and estimating the effects of concentrations because the RCC (i) places considerable reliance on market shares in making competitive assessments; (ii) does not systematically classify mergers into horizontal, vertical, or conglomerate; and (iii) relies too much on merging parties to collect information.	The Report proposes (i) a methodological guide for economic assessment of mergers and (ii) amendments to legislation to increase the role of economists and economic evidence in merger analysis; and (iii) suggests the preparation of Remedies Guidelines consistent with ICN best practices. Considering that certain types of mergers are more likely to harm the competitive process, criteria for in-depth analysis should consider if mergers are horizontal, vertical, or conglomerate. It is widely recognized that horizontal mergers are most likely to cause anticompetitive effects. Harmful effects of vertical mergers are usually limited to market foreclosure or facilitation of collusion. Generally, from the economic perspective, conglomerate mergers are not seen as causing competition concerns.	The Guide for Economic Analysis of Mergers proved to be a useful tool for the RCC's Economic Analysis Group, providing a reference framework for using our internal methodologies for economic analysis in merger cases (for example, unilateral effect analysis using Upward Price Pressure and Gross Upward Price Pressure).

table continues next page

Component 1: Review of the legal and regulatory framework governing market competition

	Problem	Description of the problem	Deliverable to address the problem	Changes implemented
1.3.2.a Comments to anticompetitive practices: leniency	Limited cost savings for consumers associated with cartel detection due to insufficient incentives for whistleblowers to disclose cartels.	The leniency program is not fully developed, since at the moment leniency applicants are not exempted from potential criminal prosecution. Moreover, the leniency instrument currently applied has also important gaps: (i) it adopts narrow definitions of the conditions to grant immunity; (ii) it lacks an efficient Marker System; (iii) it provides an unclear definition of "aggravating agreements" and (iv) it is unclear in terms of the ring leader's eligibility for leniency.	Comments on RCC's leniency regulations to increase legal certainty by developing cooperation with the criminal courts and refining the design of the leniency program by (i) limiting leniency to hard-core cartels; (ii) restructuring the Instructions in a way that allows for an easy and quick identification of the main elements of the leniency program; (iii) setting forth more stringent requirements to qualify for leniency and more complete requirements for the execution of the leniency agreement and (iv) improving the procedural part of the leniency process.	The new Leniency Guidelines draft incorporating the World Bank's comments has been approved by the Board and cleared by the Legislative Council. Nonetheless, its adoption has been postponed due to certain legal issues regarding pending cases that need to be addressed first.
1.3.2.b Comments on Regulations and Guidelines for the application of cease and desist commitments	Lack of opportunity to reduce costs associated with deterrence of anticompetitive practices.	RCC ability to use settlements must include the ability to negotiate the overall amount of the fine, not only the percentage of the fine reduction. Enhancing RCC flexibility to reach settlements can speed up closing investigations and allow RCC to focus its resources on those cases where economic harm is greater (settlement can be reserved for those instances where economic harm is marginal).	Comments to the Romanian 2010 Commitment Guidelines, (i) suggesting the introduction of a complementary and specific legal regime for the RCC to agree with the violators on the amount of the fine owed in cases where they acknowledge the practice they have committed and are willing to accept a fine (with some bargaining possible on its amount) and (ii) proposing several amendments and clarifications to RCC's Instructions on Commitments.	Modification of part 35 of the Instructions by expressly mentioning (i) the applicant's right to be informed of the results of the market test; (ii) his right to make any observations when the investigation was triggered by a complaint, and (iii) an extension of the deadline by which third parties may submit comments.

table continues next page

Table B.1 RAS Deliverables (continued)

Component 1: Review of the legal and regulatory framework governing market competition

	Problem	Description of the problem	Deliverable to address the problem	Changes implemented
1.3.2.c and 1.3.2.d: Fining regulations and Guidelines	High costs associated with RCC fines that are not always and necessarily proportionate to the anticompetitive behavior.	The amount of the fines issued by the RCC should reflect more closely the harm caused by the violation. For instance, RCC calculates the fines on the basis of global turnover rather than local turnover/affected markets, mitigating circumstances are many times not taken into account and onerous minimum fines prevent closing non-priority cases quickly.	Draft fining guidelines, including (i) a criterion to adjust the baseline for gravity linking the "affected turnover" with the "total turnover" of the undertaking; (ii) specification of a number of additional aggravating and mitigating factors; (iii) the possibility to adjust the fine on the basis of proportionality; (iv) the discretion of the RCC to calculate the amount of fines in special cases such as bid rigging, and (v) RCC's obligation to review these Guidelines after three years.	
1.3.3: Internal Guidance on assessment of public support for infrastructure deployment of broadband networks	Lack of connectivity and coverage for businesses in isolated areas and increased risk of administrative discretion and market distortions through the award of state aid for broadband network deployment.	Absence of analytical guidance that helps state aid–granting authorities to achieve a faster rate of broadband coverage and penetration while maintaining a level playing field between operators.	To tackle the competition concerns, public support to broadband infrastructure should (i) not undermine private sector's incentives to invest by focusing on those areas where market operators have already invested or would normally choose to invest; (ii) ensure open access to broadband infrastructure to foster downstream competition, and (iii) lower the administrative burden by using alternative means of support which do not amount to state aid (for example, compensation for a service of general economic interest (SGEI), noncommercial operations that can be used at no cost and PPP).	The RCC-approved Guidelines on the assessment of public support for broadband networks infrastructure deployment in 2014, based on the RAS recommendations.

table continues next page

Table B.1 RAS Deliverables (*continued*)

table continues next page

Component 1: Review of the legal and regulatory framework governing market competition

	Problem	Description of the problem	Deliverable to address the problem	Changes implemented
1.3.4: Methodological guide for assessing the impact of granted state aid under current state aid legislation	Increased risk of administrative discretion and market distortions associated with systematic understanding of the potential effects and impact on the market.	The lack of ex ante and ex post evaluations does not allow (i) granting authority to perform a balancing test prior to awarding the aid, which will prove the compatibility of such aid; (ii) measuring the effectiveness of the aid in a way that provides a clear and objective justification for public spending that can also be used to improve the efficiency of future public interventions.	Methodological guide to advise the different granting authorities on how to carry out ex ante and ex post assessments of state aid measures. A functional ex post evaluation involves the following steps: (i) verify the ex ante assumptions that led to state aid approval; use performance indicators; (ii) assess the effectiveness of delivering stated objectives; (iii) assess unforeseen negative impacts and propose remedies; and (iv) improve the design of schemes by taking these negative impacts into account. The guide describes the dynamic nature of state aid impact assessment and proposes a checklist to help the granting authorities carry out their economic assessment.	
1.3.5: Quick Guide on Quantitative tools for defining relevant market	Increased risk of significant costs for consumers and private sector associated with erroneous enforcement of the Competition Law in case of abusive conducts, mergers and so on.	A review of several merger decisions made by the RCC indicates that a proper market definition is seldom performed. In particular, they do not present a systematic analysis of the evidence relevant to a determination of what the relevant product was and if there were any close substitutes. It is also unclear in most cases what evidence was relied upon in arriving at a determination of the relevant geographic market.	Guide addressed to economists and case handlers in charge of performing economic analysis of markets for antitrust cases. The Guide (i) addresses the role of market definition and of quantitative techniques, including their applicability and limitations; (ii) presents two sets of quantitative techniques applied to price analysis and demand- substitutability analysis, respectively, illustrated with examples and data requirements; and (iii) analyzes a number of examples that apply the techniques described to the definition of the relevant product's geographic market.	

Table B.1 RAS Deliverables *(continued)*

Component 1: Review of the legal and regulatory framework governing market competition	Problem	Description of the problem	Deliverable to address the problem	Changes implemented
1.3.6: Guide on the analysis of effects of abuse of dominant position toward consumers	Increased risk of significant costs for consumers associated with exclusionary conduct	The lack of assessment of the effects of exclusionary practices on consumers means that the impact on consumer welfare of specific business practices is not used to determine (i) the admissibility of a complaint, to evaluate the decision to initiate an ex-officio investigation or to prioritize between cases and allocate resources accordingly and (ii) if a practice is anticompetitive and consequently should be prohibited.	Deliverable 1.3.6 presents a methodology, drawing on the EU framework and international best practices, to analyze the effects on competition and consumer welfare of (i) predation; (ii) loyalty rebates; (iii) exclusive dealing; (iv) refusal to supply and margin squeeze; and (v) bundling/tying. The expected outcome is that RCC replaces the prevailing legality tests that tend to assume that any restriction to competition by dominant firms will harm consumers, with a sound economic analysis that privileges the interventions based upon a consumer welfare criterion.	
1.3.7: Quick guide on public procurement rules and competition	Risk of inefficient public spending associated with rigged procurement procedures.	Public officials issuing public tenders lack guidance on how to apply a competition filter to the design of the procurement terms. Guidance on how to approach public-tender design from a competition angle would enhance competitive tension among bidders and reduce the risks (formation/endurance) of bid-rigging cartels.	In order to complement RCC efforts to support a more competitive public procurement policy in Romania, the World Bank provided guidelines targeting public bodies that design and issue tenders. These guidelines include detailed practical advice on each of the procurement phases: (i) prebidding: how to ensure the selection of the most pro-competitive procurement procedure; (ii) bidding design: how to design the terms of the tender to favor competition; (iii) in the bidding stage: how to maintain price at the core of the tender award; and (iv) in postbidding: how to limit contract modifications and extensions that may be restrictive of competition.	

table continues next page

Table B.1 RAS Deliverables (*continued*)

table continues next page

Component 1: Review of the legal and regulatory framework governing market competition	*Problem*	*Description of the problem*	*Deliverable to address the problem*	*Changes implemented*
1.3.8: Guidelines on electronic communications **1.3.8a: Review of the network-sharing agreements**	Increased costs for businesses and inefficient use of RCC's resources deriving from the lack of guidance on the effects of network-sharing agreements in wireless broadband markets.	RCC's analytical capacities to analyze network sharing agreements must be strengthened in order to properly balance their pro-competitive and anticompetitive effects.	The main objective of Deliverable 1.3.8 was to provide the RCC and ANCOM with guidelines that strengthen the way Competition law is applied to network-sharing agreements in Romania. The Guidelines analyze the implications of infrastructure-sharing agreements on Competition Law in light of the degree of cooperation between the parties: (i) typically, passive infrastructure-sharing agreements raise fewer competition concerns than active sharing because they do not require the sharing of network elements, do not result in the high commonality of costs and do not involve significant information and forecasting exchanges between competitors; (ii) in active infrastructure agreements the degree of cooperation increases, which raises the risk of collusion. In addition, other factors should be taken into consideration in assessing network sharing's competition risks, including (iii) the geographic scope of the agreement; (iv) the market power of the operators; (v) the duration of the agreement and (vi) the parties' commercial independence.	RCC adopted Guidelines in 2014 on network-sharing agreements offering a framework for the assessment of passive and active sharing of infrastructure.

Table B.1 RAS Deliverables (*continued*)

Component 1: Review of the legal and regulatory framework governing market competition

Problem	Description of the problem	Deliverable to address the problem	Changes implemented
1.3.9.a. Amendments to the Government Ordinance 89/2003 **1.3.9.b. Overview of the EU legislative framework and Overview of the main infringement proceedings in the railway sector**	Not fully efficient functioning of the railways market; insufficient accounting separation between rail infrastructure and railways services	The railways legislation lacked clarity and guidance on the following features: (i) scope of the powers and competences of the RSC; (ii) RSC's access charges for rail tracks and related services and (iii) compensation of public service contracts for passenger rail services.	Proposals with amendments to Romanian railways in line with EU law: (i) extending the powers and competences of the RSC; (ii) extending the services to be provided by the infrastructure manager; (iii) increasing transparency for entering the railway market; (iv) strengthening the "financial structure" of the railways sector; (v) requiring more accurate infrastructure charging rules and (vi) providing guidance on the determination of compensation for public-service contracts.	The Recommendations made were adopted through Government Ordinance 12/2014 on modifying Law 11/1990 on fighting unfair competition in August 2014. Ordinance 12/2004 incorporates core RAS recommendations, including an "opportunity test" to trigger RCC's competence (that is, public interest or the market structure must be affected) and a general, unfair competition law catch-all clause. Furthermore, it offers a clearer definition of the purpose of the law and aligns the terminology used with EU law. In addition to Ordinance 12/2014, the RCC enacted a Procedural Regulation in November 2014, which clarifies the opportunity test and issues of capacity to submit complaints with the RCC.
1.3.10.a. and 1.3.10.b. **Regulatory clarifications on the Unfair Competition legal framework**	RCC's resources are inefficiently used due to the lack of case prioritization.	Inconsistent approach to unfair competition with loopholes between different pieces of legislation, unclear definition of the competence of RCC vis-à-vis other agencies and both civil and criminal jurisdictions and the lack of criteria to prioritize RCC's intervention.	Proposal of several amendments, including (i) a general law on unfair competition applicable to all B2B activities; (ii) clear definition of RCC's competences based on an appreciability and an opportunity test and (iii) a consistent approach toward Unfair Competition Law in order to avoid loopholes between different pieces of legislation.	

table continues next page

Table B.1 RAS Deliverables *(continued)*

Component 1: Review of the legal and regulatory framework governing market competition

	Problem	Description of the problem	Deliverable to address the problem	Changes implemented
1.3.11: Clarifications on the State aid regulations	Risk of inefficient use of RCC's resources resulting from a not fully efficient State aid procedural framework that is not fully in line with the European Commission's State aid Action Plan.	Overlaps and contradictions between the Draft Procedural law and EU regulations that are directly applicable in Romania.	In order to avoid conflicts with EU law, it is suggested that the Draft law omit Articles that repeat wholly or partially provisions and definitions of EU law that are directly applicable in Romania.	WB recommendations were assessed and taken into account and discussed prior to the enactment of the Emergency Ordinance 77/2014 on State aid national procedures.
1.4: Revision of protocols signed by the Romanian Competition Council	Risk of higher costs for private sector and an inefficient use of RCC's resources vis-à-vis sectoral regulators in the application of the Competition Law.	Lack of (i) a model protocol with companion material such as a checklist to spot suspicious behavior related to anticompetitive practices; (ii) a list of indicators to monitor effective market competition and (iii) a questionnaire to assess if proposed regulations could have negative effects on competition.	Report (i) reviewing existing protocols signed by the RCC; (ii) assessing their scope on the basis of international experience and the local context; (iii) presenting recommendations on actions to strengthen the contents and utilization of the protocols; and (iv) introducing a Proposed Structure of Model Protocol. The proposed draft protocols suggest a more effective regulatory framework to enact cooperation on the basis of (i) enhanced consultation mechanisms in the context of merger analysis, State aid and unfair commercial practices; (ii) consistent procedural rules for bearance, confidentiality, information sharing, periodical meetings, focal points, confidentiality, allocation of cases and transferring cases to the competent authority and (iii) a periodical review to ensure that the content of the protocol is current and that the parties maintain an interest in its implementation.	

table continues next page

69

Table B.1 RAS Deliverables *(continued)*

Component 1: Review of the legal and regulatory framework governing market competition

	Problem	Description of the problem	Deliverable to address the problem	Changes implemented
1.4.1: Draft Protocol between the RCC and ANRE and Recommendations for an Action Plan	Risk of higher costs for private sector and an inefficient use of RCC's resources vis-à-vis sectoral regulators in the application of the Competition Law in the electricity sector.	Lack of specific provisions in the Protocol related to market inquiries and State aid in the electricity sector and of an action plan setting out detailed steps to implement the Protocol.	Proposal of changes to the framework of cooperation between RCC and ANRE have been taken into consideration as the protocol has been updated and the action plan was agreed on, including (i) a revised Protocol for Cooperation with a timetable of activities and goals as well as mechanisms to share expertise; (ii) periodic meetings where the short-term, medium-term, and long-term needs of each agency and also of the Romanian economy are discussed and incorporated into a shared vision; (iii) definition of the role of each organization; (iv) joint market inquiries led by the RCC every four to five years; (v) access by the RCC to the information collected under the REMIT framework and (vi) the development of a common approach to State aid in the electricity sector.	
1.4.2: Protocol between the RCC and ANCOM	Risk of higher costs for private sector and an inefficient use of RCC's resources vis-à-vis sectoral regulators in the application of the Competition Law in the telecommunications sector.	Limited specific provisions in the Protocol in relation to ex ante and ex post intervention in telecommunications markets and of an action plan setting out detailed steps to implement the Protocol.	Proposal of amendments to the Protocol signed in 2010 between RCC and the ANCOM and creation of an action plan have been addressed by the two institutions by updating the protocol with the proposed action plan which included (i) strengthening the mechanisms for consultation and information exchange in cases of sectoral investigations and preliminary investigations; (ii) consistency of hierarchical levels of appointed focal points across institutions; and (iii) the establishment of focal points comprising middle/senior management level from the main areas of collaboration.	

table continues next page

Table B.1 RAS Deliverables *(continued)*

Component 1: Review of the legal and regulatory framework governing market competition

	Problem	Description of the problem	Deliverable to address the problem	Changes implemented
1.4.3: Draft Model protocol with the National Agency for Medicines (ANM)	Risk of higher costs for private sector and an inefficient use of RCC's resources vis-à-vis sectoral regulators in the application of the Competition Law in the pharmaceuticals sector.	Lack of a specific framework to implement the inter-agency cooperation. Moreover, key topics where cooperation needs to be operationalized such as unfair commercial practices and merger control are not included in the Protocol.	The framework of cooperation between the RCC and the ANM must be updated according to European and international best practices, particularly in terms of (i) enhanced collaboration tools including periodic and ad hoc consultations and obligation to notify investigations; (ii) identification of focal points to centralize communication; (iii) inclusion of a specific provision dealing with information sharing and confidentiality issues and (iv) cooperation in the field of unfair commercial practices.	
1.4.4: Draft Model protocol with the Insurance Supervisory Commission (part of Financial Surveillance Authority)	Risk of higher costs for private sector and an inefficient use of RCC's resources vis-à-vis sectoral regulators in the application of the Competition Law in the insurance sector.	Lack of a specific framework to implement inter-agency cooperation. Moreover, key topics where cooperation is needed, such as unfair commercial practices and merger control, are not included in the Protocol.	The framework of cooperation between the RCC and the Insurance Supervisory Commission must be updated according to European and international best practices, particularly in terms of (i) enhanced collaboration tools including periodic and ad hoc consultations and obligation to notify investigations; (ii) identification of focal points to centralize communication;(iii) inclusion of a specific provision dealing with information sharing and confidentiality issues; (iv) cooperation in the field of unfair commercial practices and (v) collaboration regarding merger notifications.	

table continues next page

71

Table B.1 RAS Deliverables (*continued*)

Component 1: Review of the legal and regulatory framework governing market competition

	Problem	Description of the problem	Deliverable to address the problem	Changes implemented
1.4.5: Draft Model protocol with the National Securities Commission	Risk of higher costs for private sector and an inefficient use of RCC's resources vis-à-vis sectoral regulators in the application of the Competition Law in the securities sector.	Lack of a specific framework to implement inter-agency cooperation. Moreover, key topics where cooperation is needed, such as merger control, are not included in the Protocol.	The framework of cooperation between the RCC and the Insurance National Securities Commission must be updated according to European and international best practices, particularly in terms of (i) enhanced collaboration tools including periodic and ad hoc consultations and obligation to notify investigations; (ii) identification of focal points to centralize communication; (iii) inclusion of a specific provision dealing with information sharing and confidentiality issues; (iv) cooperation in the field of unfair commercial practices; and (v) collaboration regarding merger notifications.	
1.4.6: Draft Model protocol with the National Regulatory Authority for Municipal Services (ANRSC)	Risk of higher costs for private sector and an inefficient use of RCC's resources vis-à-vis sectoral regulators in the application of the Competition Law in the area of municipal services.	Lack of a specific framework to implement inter-agency cooperation. Moreover, key topics where cooperation is needed, such as State aid, are not included in the Protocol.	The framework of cooperation between the RCC and the Insurance National Securities Commission must be updated according to European and international best practices, particularly in terms of (i) enhanced collaboration tools, including periodic and ad hoc consultations and obligation to notify investigations; (ii) identification of focal points to centralize communication; (iii) inclusion of a specific provision dealing with information sharing and confidentiality issues; (iv) cooperation in the field of unfair commercial practices and (v) cooperation in the field of State aid.	

table continues next page

Table B.1 RAS Deliverables *(continued)*

Component 1: Review of the legal and regulatory framework governing market competition

	Problem	Description of the problem	Deliverable to address the problem	Changes implemented
1.4.7: Draft Model protocol with the National Regulatory Authority for Public Procurement (ANRMAP)	Risk of higher costs for consumers and public and private sectors and an inefficient use of RCC's resources vis-à-vis sectoral regulators in the application of the Competition Law in the field of public procurement.	Lack of a specific framework to implement the inter-agency cooperation. Moreover, key topics where cooperation is needed, such as bid rigging, are not included in the Protocol.	The framework of cooperation between the RCC and the ANRMAP needs to be updated according to European and international best practices, particularly in terms of (i) enhanced collaboration tools including periodic and ad hoc consultations and obligation to notify investigations; (ii) identification of focal points to centralize communication;(iii) inclusion of a specific provision dealing with information sharing and confidentiality issues; (iv) cooperation in the field of unfair commercial practices and (v) cooperation in order to identify bidding patterns.	
1.4.8: Draft Model protocol with the National Consumer Protection Authority (ANPC)	Risk of higher costs for private sector and an inefficient use of RCC's resources vis-à-vis sectoral regulators in the application of the Competition Law in the field of consumer protection.	Lack of a specific framework to implement inter-agency cooperation. Moreover, key topics where cooperation is needed, such as unfair commercial practices, are not included in the Protocol.	The framework of cooperation between the RCC and the ANPC has been updated according to European and international best practices and WB recommendations related in particular on the need for (i) enhanced collaboration tools including periodic and ad hoc consultations and obligation to notify investigations; (ii) identification of focal points to centralize communication; (iii) inclusion of a specific provision dealing with information sharing and confidentiality issues and (iv) cooperation in the field of unfair commercial practices.	

table continues next page

Table B.1 RAS Deliverables *(continued)*

Component 1: Review of the legal and regulatory framework governing market competition	Problem	Description of the problem	Deliverable to address the problem	Changes implemented
1.5: Model protocol for cooperation with the Prosecutor's Office attached to the High Court of Cassation and Justice (POHCJJ)	Risk of higher costs for private sector and an inefficient use of RCC's resources vis-à-vis sectoral regulators in the application of Competition law.	Lack of specific provisions in the Protocol relating to the criminal prosecution of cartels.	The framework of cooperation between the RCC and the POHCJJ has been updated and an institutional action plan was agreed on in order to i) include further aspects of anticompetitive conduct enforcement with particular emphasis on the leniency program; (ii) improve institutional communication; (ii) develop and improve investigative techniques and proceedings and (iii) build capacity to enforce Competition law.	The new draft RCL includes provisions to further the cooperation with the POHCJJ and the Police.

Component 2: Strengthening the advocacy activity in the field of competition in public bodies and government bodies	Problem	Description of the problem	Deliverable to address the problem	Changes implemented
2.1.1 Advocacy event on Competition Policy in Public Procurement	Risk of inefficient public spending associated with uncompetitive public procurement processes	Non-systematic implementation of bid-rigging detection techniques and design of pro-competitive public procurement.	Training on (i) the development and implementation of screening techniques for the detection of bid rigging (Rosa Abrantes-Metz); and on international best practices in (ii) detecting bid rigging and (iii) designing the procurement process to reduce the risks of bid rigging in this process (OECD).	
2.1.2 Power of Advocacy: Competition Day **2.2.2 The Power of Advocacy: Best Practices in Advocacy and Communication Areas**	Risk of higher costs for the private sector stemming from the lack of clarity surrounding the application by the RCC of the TFEU's rules on competition.	Lack of clarity about the impact of the EU Competition rules in national cases of Competition Law.	Conference on the application of Articles 101 and 102 TFEU at the national level with a focus on (i) the application of EC Regulation no 1/2003; (ii) the economic approach to competition policy and (iii) the issue of preliminary rulings.	
2.1.3 Unfair Competition Law	Risk of higher costs for the private sector due to the lack of clarity on the distinction between Competition law and Unfair Competition law.	Insufficient clarity about RCC's role in dealing with Unfair Competition Law matters vis-à-vis other agencies and other matters (Competition law).	RCC advocacy event reviewing the Revised Romanian Drafts on the "Law on the Protection of Fair Competition" and focusing on (i) RCC's competences in unfair Competition Law; (ii) the process of settlement of minor offences and (iii) the protection of trade secrets.	
2.1.4. Compliance with Competition Law and leniency policy	Risk of higher costs for consumers stemming from insufficient cartel deterrence.	Lack of systematic use of outreach instruments to raise private sector's awareness about Competition law compliance and leniency programs.	Training on international best practices on (i) leniency, especially, the collaboration during the Competition agency and the leniency applicants, and (ii) the role of compliance processes in raising awareness of Competition law principles (ACM and Israel Antitrust Authority).	

table continues next page

Table B.1 RAS Deliverables *(continued)*

Component 2:
Strengthening the
advocacy activity in the
field of competition in
public bodies and
government bodies | *Problem* | *Description of the problem* | *Deliverable to address the problem* | *Changes implemented*

Component 2: Strengthening the advocacy activity in the field of competition in public bodies and government bodies	Problem	Description of the problem	Deliverable to address the problem	Changes implemented
2.2.1. Techniques for detecting cartels and cartel investigation **2.3.2. Screening of cartels**	Risk of higher costs for consumers stemming from insufficient cartel deterrence	Gaps in the implementation of cartel detection and investigative techniques.	Training on (i) the economics of collusion and damages (ii) effective cartel detection and deterrence programs; (iii) conducting dawn raids; (iv) evidentiary analysis and metadata and (v) interviewing techniques and other investigative tools (NMA and DoJ).	The cartel-screening techniques based on statistical analysis were adapted and used by the Economic Analysis Group for two separate projects: i) an internal guide for market screening and ii) a market- behavior analysis of beer producers in Romania provided for the Consumption Goods Directorate's beer market inquiry
2.2.3 The recent "state aid modernisation" reform and its new substantive and procedural rules	Risk of higher costs for the private sector stemming from the lack of clarity surrounding the application by the RCC of the TFEU's rules on competition.	Lack of clarity about the impact of the European Union Competition rules in national cases of State aid. New legislation will provide Romanian Government with new attributions especially in relation to i) a single national contact authority, providing advice and special assistance to national authorities and beneficiaries; ii) ensuring their adequate information about EU State aid law and policies; iii) dialoguing with the European Commission; iv) providing reports to the Government and v) collaborating with other national authorities in cases before the EU Court of Justice.	Training on: (i) What is State aid and how can it support national policies?; ii) Substantive and procedural State aid rules: public objectives can be accepted as compatible with the internal market and the roles of the different actors in State aid control (European Commission, Member States and local authorities, companies, courts)	The training helped in clarifying the concepts on EU State aid which were later used in fine-tuning the draft Emergency Ordinance 77 on State aid national procedures.

table continues next page

Table B.1 RAS Deliverables (*continued*)

Component 2:
Strengthening the
advocacy activity in the
field of competition in
public bodies and
government bodies

	Problem	Description of the problem	Deliverable to address the problem	Changes implemented
2.3.1 IT Forensics Tech-niques	Risk of higher costs for consumers stemming from insufficient cartel deterrence.	Gaps in the implementation of investigative techniques using IT Forensics tools.	Training by the DoJ on (i) extracting and seizing electronic data during dawn raids and (ii) the practical use of IT forensic tools (FTK).	
2.3.3 The new Unfair Competition Law	Risk of higher costs for the private sector due to the lack of clarity on the distinction between Competition law and Unfair Compe-tition law.	Need of enhanced clarity about RCC's role in dealing with Unfair Compe-tition Law matters vis-à-vis other agencies, procedural aspects of unfair competition cases and pos-sible interpretation of substantive concepts in the law.	Training on the systematic legal overview of The Unfair Competition Law No. 11/1991 after Ordonanta 12/2014 and after implementation of RCC Regulation on the procedure for identifying and sanctioning of unfair competition practices.	It provided for the territorial offices of RCC very informative sessions that clarified their role in detecting and investigating unfair competition practices.

Table B.1 RAS Deliverables *(continued)*

Component 3	Problem	Description of the problem	Deliverable to address the problem	Changes implemented*
3.1. Detailed Business Architecture—Current and Target	Inefficient use of RCC's resources due to an incomplete business architecture.	RCC's incomplete business architecture is shown by (i) the limited internal and external transparency; (ii) limited operational effectiveness and complex organizational processes; (iii) misalignment of the staff's roles with institutional objectives and (iv) bundling of investigative and adjudicative functions and absence of clear rules for accountability.	Business architecture that defines an optimal model for RCC without constraints by (i) improving internal and external transparency; (ii) enhancing operational effectiveness through simplified organizational processes; (iii) aligning the roles of staff with institutional objectives; (iv) separating investigative from adjudicative functions; (v) providing clear rules for accountability and (vi) pushing responsibilities to the lowest operational level.	Merger processes streamlined include (i) simplified procedures based on specific thresholds; (ii) standardized preliminary and official notification steps; (iii) deadlines which are systematized in accordance with EU practices; (iv) workloads which are distributed in accordance with pre-determined criteria; (v) accountability which is delegated to the lowest level in the process; (vi) standardized checklists and forms which are implemented to promote consistency across the RCC. RCC governance will be improved with the following amendments to the RCL: (i) separation of adjudication from investigation; (ii) new provisions regarding conflict of interest; (iii) automation of the registry by the Hearing Officer; (iv) delegation of powers from the President and (v) reassignment of operational responsibilities to the lowest possible level of the organization.

table continues next page

Table B.1 RAS Deliverables *(continued)*

Component 3	Problem	Description of the problem	Deliverable to address the problem	Changes implemented*
3.2. Target State Technology Architecture	Inefficient use of RCC's resources due to an incomplete IT architecture.	RCC's incomplete architecture manifests itself by a generalized minimal use of IT tools across RCC and the absence of IT strategies, principles, processes or architectures to define how IT can be leveraged to support business operations.	An IT strategy must be developed and anchored in a comprehensive definition of the scope and business objectives of the RCC; an IT governance framework must provide strategic guidance and ensure that IT investments and operations align with institutional priorities and IT processes and procedures must be standardized. A corporate function is necessary to manage and administer RCC's IT.	IT forensics strengthened with new technologies and requisite training in the use of these technologies. Complete case management for mergers and a start-up phase for case management of RCC's other functions: (i) data center implemented in STS; (ii) performance metrics for merger and (iii) security profiles for merger case managers.
3.3. Target State Solution architecture and Migration Plan	Inefficient use of RCC's resources by virtue of the lack of a coherent and comprehensive architecture.	There is neither a solution architecture nor a migration plan, which would take into account the recommendations of both the business and architecture plans.	A phased approach to four core reform areas (strategy, governance, mandated functions and technology) were recommended and synthesized in a migration plan. The recommendations include (i) a new strategy, advocacy and communication unit will support the RCC Board in defining its annual strategy; (ii) commissioners may delegate powers according to a pre-defined criteria; (iii) RCC will focus on public interest antitrust and merger cases and (iv) financial and human resources management will be supported by common IT.	Strategy: (i) Management information on merger activities is made available through reports and management dashboard. (ii) monitoring and performance evaluation of merger activities and its alignment with the overall strategic framework can be tracked in real-time. Governance: (i) Accountabilities and responsibilities are now clearly defined and managed systematically, that is, RCC staff who should only be informed of activities have only view access to screens and cannot edit the data; (ii) an IT Governance Framework was operationalized with the establishment of a Steering Committee composed of mid-level management.

table continues next page

Table B.1 RAS Deliverables *(continued)*

Component 3	Problem	Description of the problem	Deliverable to address the problem	Changes implemented*
				Mandated function: Standard registration process was created as a separate service and will be reused for all other RCC processes.
3.4: Enterprise Architecture Method Guide	Inefficient use of RCC's resources due to the lack of a coherent and comprehensive enterprise- architecture methodology to be used within the organization.	The RCC must take a holistic view of the enterprise at a strategic level and then use it to plan and execute the architecture definition, plan the migrations to the target state and implement them according to the architectures and releases defined.	An Enterprise Architecture (EA) Methodology contributes toward defining a target state enterprise architecture for an organization through a comprehensive and holistic approach that takes into account the institution's strategic planning (business, ITC, communication) and its governance. The methodology described in the deliverable leverages methods, frameworks and models from several industry-standard architecture methodologies, including the Zachman Framework, The Open Group Architecture Framework (TOGAF), and the Architecture Definition Process used at World Bank.	The methodology will help the RCC internal project-management unit while implementing the next steps of the target architecture and will support greater engagement with RCC internal core business stakeholders to define, implement and manage business rules and policies for their respective business areas.

* This first release is scheduled to be launched by the end of March 2015.

Table B.1 RAS Deliverables (continued)

Component 4	Problem	Description of the problem	Deliverable to address the problem	Changes implemented
4.1. Training needs assessment	Inefficient use of RCC's resources due to insufficient capacity building to address core functions.	(i) No structured approach to staff planning linked to the RCC strategy; (ii) not fully efficient recruitment and selection processes; (iii) no structured process in place for induction; (iv)/not sufficient transparency in terms of grade promotion; (v) inefficient performance- evaluation process;(vi) non-systematic approach to the staff development approach to communications with employees; (viii) insubstantial talent management processes; (ix) limited strategic role of HR Directorate on organizational development and (x)need to allocate more resources and enhance management and organizational capacities of the HR Directorate.	Strengthening of the recruitment and selection processes, namely through (i) a greater involvement of the HR Manager and the ANFP representatives; (ii) trainings in recruitment techniques and (iii) use of key performance indicators for the recruitment process; (iii)/designing and implementing a successful induction/ onboarding process; (iv) creating greater transparency in the process of grade promotion and building a set of performance indicators; (v) improving processes for setting staff objectives and performance evaluation and aligning them with RCC's mission; setting development needs in a clearer, more prioritized, and transparent way incorporating development activities in a clearly defined Development Strategy and building a set of key business indicators for the development process.	(i) More structured approach to staff planning in line with RCC's overall strategy; (ii) Greater human resources involvement in recruitment and selection processes and adoption of key performance indicators; (iii) adoption of an induction procedure; (iv) a more transparent approach to grade promotion (communication of promotions available during the upcoming period) and adoption of key performance indicators and (vi) creation of competencies- based profiles.
4.2. Detailed training plan	Insufficient personnel development plan.	Insufficient structured training on case competences and skills.	Detailed Training Plan (i) defining the objectives, structure and delivery method and evaluation tools for each training category and recommending measures to integrate the training policy within the HR Management Policy and HR Information Systems and (ii) proposing a detailed roadmap for its implementation.	Courses delivered by the World Bank: Deliverables 4.3.1–4.3.12.
4.3.1 Dawn Raids, Investigative Methods, Specific Instruments and Basic IT Practices and Basic IT Forensics	Inefficient use of RCC's resources due to gaps in its investigators' core skills in terms of investigative techniques and basic IT Forensics.	Insufficient targeted training in IT Forensics and investigative techniques that can be used to tackle cartels more effectively.	Workshop on "Conducting dawn raids in practice: Investigative methods and forensics analysis"	

table continues next page

Table B.1 RAS Deliverables *(continued)*

Component 4	Problem	Description of the problem	Deliverable to address the problem	Changes implemented
4.3.2 Dawn Raids, Investigative Methods and Specific Instruments and Practices and Basic IT Forensics	Inefficient use of RCC's resources due to gaps in investigative techniques and basic IT Forensics.	Insufficient targeted training in IT Forensics and investigative techniques that can be used to tackle cartels more effectively.	Workshop on "Conducting dawn raids in practice: investigative methods and forensics analysis"	
4.3.3 Comparative Competition Jurisprudence in EU Law	Undue burden for the private sector that raises the costs of doing business stemming from the lack of clarity surrounding the application by the RCC of the TFEU's rules on competition.	Insufficient in-depth training in the following core areas of EU Competition law: horizontal and vertical agreements (Article 101 TFEU), abuse of dominance (Article 102 TFEU) and merger control.	Workshop on "Comparative Competition Jurisprudence in EU Law: Intensive training course"	
4.3.4 Principles of Competition and Unfair Competition	Inefficient use of RCC's resources because of gaps between the core principles of the Unfair Competition law and those of the Competition law in the regional offices.	Insufficient specific training for the regional staff in the fundamentals of Competition law and of Unfair Competition law and limited knowledge about the European and International best practices in these fields.	Intensive training course on "Principles of Unfair and Competition Law"	
4.3.5 Economic Research and Analysis for Competition Inspectors I	Risk of higher costs for consumers and private sector stemming from gaps in economic analysis.	Insufficient targeted training in the economics behind Competition law, especially in terms of (i) market definition; (ii) identification of market power and (iii) abuse of dominance and vertical restraints.	Intensive training course on "The Economics behind Competition Law"	

table continues next page

Table B.1 RAS Deliverables (continued)

Component 4	Problem	Description of the problem	Deliverable to address the problem	Changes implemented
4.3.6 Economic Research and Analysis for Competition Inspectors II	Risk of higher costs for consumers and private sector stemming from gaps in economic analysis.	Insufficient targeted training in the economics behind Competition law, especially in terms of (i) restrictions of competition by object and restrictions by effect; (ii) pro-competitive agreements among competitors; (iii) oligopolies and collusion; (iv) merger control policy and (v) IP rights and Competition law.	Intensive training course on "The Economics behind Competition Law"	
4.3.7 Effective Written Communication on Competition Topics	Unclear RCC decisions.	Insufficient in-depth training focused on best practices in effective written communications.	Workshop on Effective Written Communications on competition topics	
4.3.8 Principles of Effective People Management and Communication	Risk of inefficient use of resources due to an inefficient framework for management and communication.	Insufficient specific training in management and communication skills.	Seminar on effective communications and finance for non-financial managers.	
4.3.9 Leadership and Problem solving for antitrust investigators	Risk of inefficient use of resources resulting from insufficient leadership and problem-solving skills.	Insufficient targeted training in problem solving in antitrust investigations.	Leadership training course	
4.3.10 Competition Project Management	Risk of inefficient use of resources resulting from poor management of competition cases.	Insufficient in-depth training in project management.	Intensive training course on "Competition Project Management"	

table continues next page

Table B.1 RAS Deliverables *(continued)*

Component 4	Problem	Description of the problem	Deliverable to address the problem	Changes implemented
4.3.11 Strategy Formulation and Change Management	Risk of inefficient use of resources resulting from the lack of strategy formulation and lack of adaptation to change management.	Insufficient specific training in strategy formulation and change management.	Workshop "For a Successful Management of Change: Balancing Performance and Strategy"	
4.3.12 Leadership and Problem Solving for Antitrust Investigators	Risk of inefficient use of resources resulting from insufficient leadership and problem-solving skills.	Insufficient in-depth training in problem solving in antitrust investigations.	Leadership training course	
4.4 Assessment of the HR capacity-building component for implementation	Risk of inefficient use of RCC's resources due to insufficient capacity building to address core functions.	(i) No structured approach to staff planning linked to the RCC strategy; (ii) /non-systematic approach to the staff development process; (iii) insufficiently structured approach to communications with employees; (iii) limited strategic role of HR Directorate in organizational development and (iv) need to allocate more resources to and enhance management and organizational capacities of the HR Directorate.	The report aims to depict the progress, as well as existing gaps and needs, in the Romanian Competition Council (RCC), in order to carry out efficiently and effectively the functional RCC activities and Human Resources capacity development. The Competency Architect Tool (CAT) is a methodology used for human resource evaluation which is based on the concept of "competency," which is defined as the triad "knowledge-skill-attitude."	Report approved by RCC Human Resources Management and used for future strategic training planning of the institution.

Note: ANCOM = National Authority for Communication; ANRE = the Energy Regulatory Agency; DoJ = Department of Justice; EU = European Union; ICN = International Competition Network; HR = Human resource; IT = information technology; NMA = Netherlands Competition Authority; OECD = Organisation for Economic Co-operation and Development; PPP = purchasing power parity; RAS = Romania Spatial and Urban Strategy Reimbursable Advisory Service; RCC = Romania Competition Council; RCL = Romanian Competition law; RSC = Railways Supervisory Council; TFEU = Treaty on the Functioning of the European Union; WB = World Bank.

Bibliography

International Competition Network (ICN). 2009. Report on the Agency Effectiveness Project: Second Phase—Effectiveness of Decisions. Presented at the 8th Annual Conference of the ICN. Zurich, June 3–5, 2009, pp. 12–13.

International Monetary Fund (IMF). 2014. World Economic Outlook database. https://www.imf.org/external/pubs/ft/weo/2014/02/weodata/index.aspx

Jolly, David. 2009. "I.M.F. Announces Financial Rescue Plan for Romania." *New York Times*, March 25. http://www.nytimes.com/2009/03/26/business/worldbusiness/26romania.html?_r=0.

Kitzmuller, Markus, and Martha Martinez Licetti. 2012. "Competition Policy: Encouraging Thriving Markets for Development." *Viewpoint: Public Policy for the Private Sector* 331 (September).

Motta, Massimo. 2004. *Competition Policy: Theory and Practice*. New York: Cambridge University Press.

Organisation for Economic Co-operation and Development (OECD), Directorate for Financial and Enterprise Affairs Competition Committee. 2013. "Recent Developments in Rail Transportation Services." Policy Roundtables. December 13. DAF/COMP (2013)24.

Romanian Competition Council. 2012. *Annual Report 2012*. Romanian Competition Council. http://www.consiliulconcurentei.ro/en/publications/annual-reports.html.

Romanian Competition Council. 2013. *Annual Report 2013*. Romanian Competition Council. http://www.consiliulconcurentei.ro/en/publications/annual-reports.html

United Nations Development Programme (UNDP) Romania. 2002. National Human Development Report. Romania 2001–2002: A Decade Later: Understanding the Transition Process in Romania. Available at http://hdr.undp.org/sites/default/files/romania_2001_en.pdf.

Voigt, S. 2009. "The Effects of Competition Policy on Development—Cross-Country Evidence Using Four New Indicators." *Journal of Development Studies* 45 (8): 1225–48.

World Bank. 2010. "Functional Review of the Romanian Competition Council." Final Report No. 74282. The World Bank Europe and Central Asia Region. October 15. Washington, DC.

World Bank. 2013a. *Reviving Romania's Growth and Convergence Challenges and Opportunities: A Country Economic Memorandum*. Report No. 74635-RO, June 21. Washington, DC: World Bank. http://documents.worldbank.org/curated/en/2013/06/18028709/reviving-romanias-growth-convergence-challenges-opportunities-country-economic-memorandum.

World Bank. 2013b. "Product Market Policies in Romania: A Comparison with EU Partners." *Policy Research Working Paper* 6698 (November).

World Bank. 2014a. Changing Mindsets to Transform Markets: Lessons Learned from the First Annual Awards in Competition Policy Advocacy. http://www.worldbank.org/en/events/2014/11/26/2014-competition-advocacy-contest.

World Bank. 2014b. *Reimbursable Advisory Services: Delivering Expertise & Customized Solutions for Our Clients.* June. http://pubdocs.worldbank.org/pubdocs/publicdoc/2014/9/789121408557919817/RAS-Brochure2014web.pdf.

Environmental Benefits Statement

green press INITIATIVE

www.ingramcontent.com/pod-product-compliance
Lightning Source LLC
Chambersburg PA
CBHW080850300326
41935CB00040B/1698